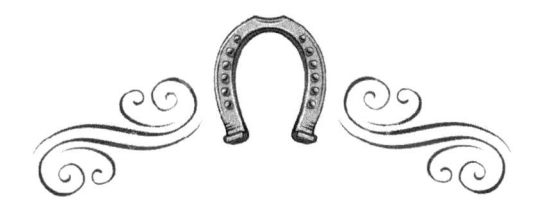

From the STREETS *of* BROOKLYN *to* TRAINER TO THE STARS

JOHN PARISELLA'S LIFETIME *of* CELEBRITY CONNECTIONS

by
DENNY DRESSMAN

HIT THE MARK BOOKS

DENVER

Copyright © 2019
Hit the Mark Books

All rights reserved.
No part of this book may be reproduced
in any form or by any means without permission
in writing from the author, except for brief quotations
embodied in critical articles and reviews.

Hit the Mark Books
P.O. Box 1181
Parker, CO 80134

hitthemarkbooks.com

ISBN 978-1-7335204-0-9
paperback

ISBN 978-1-7335204-1-6
hardcover

For my dad,

who came from nothing

but gave me everything

J. P.

Table of Contents

Paddock
Introduction 3

Starting Gate
Son of Brooklyn.. 9
Street-smart.. 17
Understanding Charlie's Boy 24
Pepi and the Yankees 30
An Unlikely Path.. 36
Campo's Protege 41
Photo Finish 45

First Turn
'Trainer to the Stars' 55
John's 'Bonnie' 64
'Bethenny Parisella' 72
Ups and Downs 83

Backstretch
Claim to Fame 97
Running for the Roses 105
The Boss 115
World Record 120
John's Jockey.. 128

Far Turn
NBA Insider 137
Bianchi's 'Beard'.. 153
Kentucky Calling... 164
Gabbysaydada 172

Homestretch
Glory Year 181
The Racing Game 190
Lifesaver.. 195

Winner's Circle
God's Odds 209
A Dream Come True 216
Family Album 220
Through Others' Eyes....................................... 222

Author's Note 225

"John's led such an incredible life – a roller-coaster life, like probably very few."

Rick Pitino

Paddock

Previous page: Bethenny Frankel, John Parisella's stepdaughter, on horseback; *(photo courtesy of Bernadette Birk)* Rick Pitino and a friend, Bob Gonzalez (center), with John *(photo courtesy of Melissa Sanders)*

Introduction

Mickey Mantle and George Steinbrenner . . . Don Rickles and James Caan . . . Rick Pitino and Bethenny Frankel . . .

What do these famous people—and dozens more—have in common? They all are part of John Parisella's lifetime of celebrity connections. They're all part of the story of one of the most colorful figures in one of history's most colorful sports.

An accomplished trainer of Thoroughbred racehorses, John Parisella grew up on the streets of post-Depression, post-war Brooklyn. The son of a bookmaker and shylock, he began playing the horses at Aqueduct and Belmont while still in high school. Afraid of horses, he nonetheless became the protégé of fellow New Yorker John Campo, one of racing's Hall of Fame trainers, and became a Hall of Fame-caliber trainer in his own right.

John Parisella ran horses at thirty-eight tracks during a career that spanned six decades, and almost half the Thoroughbreds he sent to the post finished in the money. His most famous horse, Simply Majestic, once ran faster than the great Secretariat and in the process broke Big Red's world record for the mile and an eighth. John's notable success was rooted in his unusual ability to transform also-rans into winners while also developing champions.

But that's only part of the story.

Blessed with a flamboyant personality that Damon Runyon could have created for a character in one of his novels, Parisella also enjoyed more than five decades of adventures with the biggest names in sports, entertainment and business. In the early 1970s he appeared twice on "The Tonight Show With Johnny Carson," and the second time was named the "Trainer to the Stars" by actor Jack Klugman because, at that time, Parisella was training horses for a stable of movie stars that included Klugman, Caan and Telly Savalas.

He went drinking with Mantle; cajoled Steinbrenner into helping Joe Pepitone after the by-then-retired former Yankee star was in trouble with the law; was looked after by Rickles' agent, Joe Scandore—his Italian uncle—who opened many doors in the entertainment world; lived with Caan at the height of Caan's fame; became Pitino's close friend, intermediary with the New York Knicks and behind-the-scenes orchestrator of Pitino's move to head basketball coach at the University of Kentucky; and, as Bethenny Frankel's stepfather, was the father-figure in the future Reality TV star's life growing up (only to see the relationship deteriorate in her adulthood).

> *Broadway Joe Namath ... Presidential candidate Barry Goldwater ... iconic actor James Stewart ... Bono, lead singer of the mega-group U2 ... former Kentucky Gov. Brereton Jones ... and New York City shock jock Howard Stern ...*

They, too, are among the many stars within John Parisella's almost-unimaginable orbit.

Parisella shared the Green Room with Broadway Joe and was in makeup with Jimmy Stewart before a Dean Martin Roast on television; spoke at length with Goldwater that same night; introduced Bono to Frank Sinatra in Las Vegas—which led to Sinatra including Bono in a subsequent album of songs with other vocal artists; obtained the endorsement of Pitino (arguably the most influential person in basketball-crazed

Kentucky) when Jones campaigned (successfully) for the highest elective office in the Bluegrass State; and once sold a million-dollar house to Stern.

He was even befriended by John A. Gotti, son of the man called The Teflon Don, mob boss John J. Gotti (known as John Gotti Jr.).

Parisella lived faster than his horses ran, burning through millions of dollars in ways ranging from amazing generosity to profligate spending. Diagnosed with bipolar disorder, he endured some of the addictive behaviors associated with the condition—drug abuse and compulsive gambling.

But reliance on his religious faith, including becoming a close friend of Msgr. Thomas Hartman of the God Squad television show, and the birth of his daughter Gabrielle and his devotion to her, helped turn his life around. He became a role model for others with personal challenges like those he overcame, and enjoyed his proudest moment when he walked "Gabby" down the aisle at her wedding—with her godfather, Coach Pitino, among the invited guests.

"Few training careers have twisted and turned more," one New York writer once penned. "There have been few racing comebacks anywhere as dramatic, remarkable and emotional as Parisella's," wrote another.

It takes a book to tell the whole story.

Starting Gate

Previous page: First man on the moon *(NASA photo);*
the Brooklyn Bridge with its center walkway *(Getty Images)*

Son of Brooklyn

DURING THE WORST YEARS OF The Great Depression, the Red Hook section of Brooklyn *(Roode Hoek* as Dutch settlers named it in 1636) was home to one of America's countless Hoovervilles, the name given to hundreds of shantytowns occupied by the homeless in cities across America. Life in a Hooverville was, of its nature, minimal and hard. By the time John Parisella was born in Red Hook on September 1, 1941, that Hooverville had disappeared, as had most others. But things really hadn't changed very much—not even by the time John was old enough to remember.

> *There was no neighborhood in Red Hook. I can't describe it. There was nothing there. You go outside and maybe you see an empty lot or a pile of bricks. There was no way you could play ball or anything like that.*
>
> *The big thing there was to go to the Brooklyn Boys Club, where you could play some sports. There were no areas, nothing. It was destitute.*
>
> *It was one of the poorest areas in all of Brooklyn, for sure— by far one of the poorest areas in all of Brooklyn, or the Bronx.*

A person who became world lightweight champ, Paddy DeMarco, was our next door neighbor. My dad was into boxing a lot because of him.

You had to be a certain age, but my dad was able to sneak me in to see some fights. The sad part of the story with DeMarco is that, when I was 18, 20 years old, I would go to a card game at night, and he was the dealer. He was broke.

Almost all of Red Hook's cobblestone streets have been paved over, and the only cable car to be seen in 2018 was an exhibit near one of the waterfront restaurants. But the steel fire escapes outside virtually all buildings remained—evidence that the bleak quarters occupied in the '40s by the families of Pasquale Parisella, his three brothers and a sister were as good as it got in what had been the busiest freight port in the world until container shipping came along in the 1960s.

There were no real accommodations. It was five families each trying to find a one-bedroom apartment that would work. My father's youngest brother lived with my grandmother, his mother.

We had nothing. I think we just looked for the smallest apartments and the cheapest. That's how we all lived until we finally got together and went into this one house, five families together, that was available by the Navy Yard.

John's dad Pasquale, known by all as Charlie, scraped to make ends meet when John was a boy. John got his first job at the age of six—when Charlie convinced a newspaper distributor that the young lad, despite his youth, was "an amazing go-getter." With that, John became a newsboy, delivering twenty-five copies of the *Brooklyn Eagle*. Pasquale allowed John to keep what he earned.

Ever the hustler, by the age of eight John had expanded his business enterprise, distributing a hundred copies with the help of two ten-year-olds who, he told the *Eagle* circulation representative, were "working for me." He had the paper route for four years—moving on at the age when most boys were just starting to throw the local news. From his earliest years, John was full of energy—rambunctious, some would say—and industrious while also a challenge for his struggling parents.

I worked at different jobs from the time I was six years old. I couldn't drive so I was carrying packages out to cars for older people; they'd tip me twenty-five cents. I sold Christmas trees.

Later, one of the jobs I had was pumping gas. A fancy car would pull up, and as I'm pumping gas, I'm saying to myself, "I wonder if I'll ever drive a fancy car in my life." (Porsches and Jaguars were in his future.) *Or we'd play stickball in the street and a plane would go overhead, and I'd say to myself, "Gee, I wonder if I'll ever get to ride in a plane."* (He would jet back and forth over America for decades, often on private planes.)

One of America's largest afternoon dailies when John delivered it, the *Eagle* would cease publication just a few years later, the casualty of a strike by the Newspaper Guild. But in 1951, John's last year as a newsboy, it was riding high, winner of the Pulitzer Prize for investigative reporting for an eight-part series on—of all things—illegal bookmaking and police corruption. That's a laugh in John Parisella's case because back then, Charlie was one of the many bookies who worked in Brooklyn's numerous horse rooms. Later he went on his own and became one of the biggest independent operators in New York City, eventually moving on to numbers and loan-sharking—all with the Mafia's blessing. But years of barely getting by came first.

Dad worked in the horse rooms for probably fifteen years. He was booking numbers also, which he did for a long time. He was doing that at my aunts' house. One time two of my aunts got arrested, but he didn't.

When I was, like, five years old, I was going with my father to Jamaica Race Track, one of the oldest racetracks, in Sheepshead Bay. My dad would take me there for luck. That's pretty common among Italians—superstitions ... good-luck charms.

To go from living with roaches to becoming 'Trainer To The Stars'—THAT was my big accomplishment.

A highlight of John's childhood years, he recalled, were the *johnny pumps,* the nickname for the fire hydrants in whose streams of water he and his friends frolicked on hot summer days.

My best memories are when I had nothing—when I couldn't afford to go to a pool and we would turn on the fire hydrant in our bathing suits and that was our swimming, and the cops came. Memories like that are the greatest memories in my life. I have memories, like the Brooklyn Dodgers, that just don't stop.

* * *

THE YEARS OF JOHN'S YOUTHFUL ENTRY into the newspaper business and the *Eagle's* heyday were the glory years of Snider, Hodges, Campy and Jackie, of Newk and Skoonj, Preacher and Pee Wee—of "dem Bums" and The Boys of Summer: the Dodgers.

From 1947 through 1956, Brooklyn hung six National League pennants at cozy Ebbets Field, the big league ballpark crammed into a single city block bounded by Bedford Avenue, Sullivan Place and McKeever and Montgomery Streets in Crown Heights (or, some said, Flatbush). It would have been seven if Philly's Whiz Kids hadn't thrown out the deciding run in the bottom of the ninth then scored the winner in the tenth of the last game of the 1950 season. And it could have been eight if not for what the incomparable Red Smith named the "Miracle of Coogan's Bluff"—when "dem Bums" squandered a 13 ½-game lead in the last 50 games in 1951 then lost a three-game playoff to their arch rivals, the New York Giants, on the last swing of the third game—Bobby Thomson's "Shot Heard 'Round The World," a three-run homer off Ralph Branca with one out in the bottom of the ninth that overcame a 4-2 Dodger lead. (In 1955 the Dodgers finally won the World Series, beating the Yankees in seven games.)

Those years were also the time of "The Dodger Sym-PHONY Band" and Happy Felton's Knothole Gang. (Felton, a local bandleader, vaudeville actor and early television personality hosted his Knothole Gang show from right field twenty-five minutes before each home game. Three young fans would warm up in the bullpen then compete for a solo chat with a Dodgers player the next day.)

For almost two decades, the ragtag Sym-PHONY (emphasis on the latter syllables) played at every home game, razzing the umpires with "Three Blind Mice" and serenading the players with a variety of tunes and sounds appropriate to the moment, including Armand Soriano's crashing cymbals when someone plopped down on the dugout bench. The Sym-PHONY had its own row in Section 8 (known fondly as the "loco section") and members were admitted free, by order of club president and general manager Branch Rickey.

Band member Shorty Larese lived across the street from John and was the little boy's ride to Ebbets Field from Red Hook, as well as his ticket to the games.

My father couldn't afford to pay for baseball tickets. But I was able to get in with Shorty every day for nothing, so I saw every game. He was like family, a close friend.

Through it all, young John Parisella was the team's Number One Fan. *LIFE* magazine said so.

I'd enter with the band; I'd be part of the band. That's why LIFE magazine, which was one of the biggest magazines back then, did an article about the band and mentioned my name as being the biggest Brooklyn Dodger fan. I was very vociferous, yelling at the umps and doing this and that.

I was, like, six years old in 1947. You really appreciated baseball more in those years at a very young age than you do today. At least that's my feeling. I was aware of Jackie Robinson, but I didn't understand. I wasn't able to absorb the whole thing. I remember people balking at it, but he was a good ballplayer. That's all I cared about.

After he finished eighth grade at Sacred Heart School, John and his parents moved to the Brooklyn Navy Yard neighborhood, "which was better than where we were." That's when the families of the five siblings shared one house.

During the war years, the Brooklyn Navy Yard became the nation's foremost producer of warships, and the pedestrian walkways on the Williamsburg and Manhattan Bridges over the East River, which afforded good overhead views of the 200-acre Yard, were enclosed to prevent espionage. Many of the surrounding residences were just humble walkup apartments then—not fashionable and upscale brownstones, as they would be known and marketed sixty to seventy years later.

When we moved to the Brooklyn Navy Yard area, all the buildings had stoops and people would sit outside. They would call it a block, like between Clinton Avenue and Myrtle Avenue. The next block was Vanderbilt Avenue.

Everybody would sit on the stoop because everybody knew each other. There was no stranger on the block.

The thought of those stoops triggered a memory in John that paints a vivid picture of his life growing up in Brooklyn.

> *I was 12 or 13 years old and I was playing cards on a stoop with guys who were 16 and 17. My father was passing by, because we lived, like, four houses down, and he stopped the car and ran up and took me by the neck and told those guys, "If I ever see you with him again, you're going to answer to me."*
>
> *Naturally, I didn't listen. We played under a lamppost—lampposts were big in our neighborhood.*
>
> *My father catches me again. I go running and he catches me. He brings me upstairs and says, "What did I tell you?"*
>
> *I said, "You ruined me because I was winning. I'm beating these guys."*
>
> *He lifts me up in the air and there was a hook on the wall. I was hanging on a hook. My mother had to take me down.*

There's another part of John's youth that was quintessentially part of growing up in Brooklyn: Louie's Candy Store.

> *Louie's Candy Store played such a significant role in my life from the age of thirteen to seventeen. It was an education for me, being there.*
>
> *Louie was a real character, and everybody liked to break his balls. Louie's veins would pop out. He was a thin, old man, gray hair.*
>
> *There were about eight girls and ten guys, from different schools or just the neighborhood; some of the guys didn't go to school. "One Summer Night" by The Danleers was F1 on the jukebox.*

"One Summer Night" was released in May 1958 by a small Brooklyn recording studio. It became so popular regionally that AMP 3 Records leased the song to Mercury Records for national release. It sold over a million copies. The Danleers, five guys from Brooklyn who started out singing on street corners under lampposts as so many groups did then, were one-hit wonders who eventually disbanded.

That's when I was in love with Jeanie. But she had a tough guy she would see once in a while. His name was Bubby; he wasn't a regular.

I went out of my way to make sure the tough guy liked me, because I had a crush on Jeanie. The purpose was to get her to go to the prom with me. (She did.)

Louie's Candy Store was the home of Egg Creams—that foamy fountain drink containing neither egg nor cream but rather, seltzer water, milk and syrup (usually chocolate). "It represents Brooklyn," John said, "the No. 1 drink in Brooklyn for 40 years." (National Egg Cream Day is March 15.)

Louie's also was the site of countless rank-out contests, those adolescent rituals in which boys would challenge each other with insults about their attire, appearance or intelligence, the last retort deciding each round's winner. "Someone would ask something like, 'where'd you get those fruity shoes,'" John said, "and you'd have to be able to have an answer."

In many ways, life at Louie's Candy Store helps to explain the colorful figure John Parisella became.

Street-smart

IN THE EARLY 1950s BROOKLYN—with its more than forty neighborhoods—was a melting pot of almost 2.7 million ethnically diverse residents, making it easily the most populous of New York City's boroughs, and rivaling Chicago, America's second-largest city, in total population. The groundbreaking stage play *West Side Story* wasn't set in Brooklyn, but it could have been. And hyperactive, street-wise John Parisella easily could have been one of its leading characters.

With so many Italians, Irish, Germans, African-Americans, Hispanics, European Jews and other ethnic groups sharing space, some neighborhoods weren't so neighborly. Inevitably, there were numerous tough parts of town. John recalls Fort Greene Park, not far from where he lived, as one of the toughest.

Named for General Nathaniel Greene, a hero of the American Revolution, Fort Greene Park sits on part of the high ground where the Continental Army built fortifications in preparation for the Battle of Long Island. Eighteen years into the 21st Century the thirty-acre park had become a place where sunbathers spread blankets in the grass, mothers pushed baby strollers, and groups of children enjoyed day trips. But it wasn't that way when John was growing up.

> *At that time it was like you saw in the movies—there were big fights in Fort Greene Park. There was a white gang, a black gang and a Spanish gang. They did damage to white boys. One time I had a knife to my neck; another time I faced a gun in a car with a Spanish guy. I took some beatings.*

(One time) these black guys attacked myself and my friend. Why? Because we were white. They tied us up with chains and we actually hung by chains. Our people were worried about us and they kept searching. We hung there a coupla hours before they found us; it wasn't that they found us in five minutes.

That was my life. So I really had to make it a point—and thank goodness I was likeable—to make friends with the leader of each gang.

I was a survivor. I would get in fights and lose; if I had a hundred fights, I lost ninety-eight of them. But I was unafraid.

When John was on the edge of his teen years, the leader of the white gang, the Forty Thieves, posed a particularly daunting dare: twenty bucks (equal to almost $200 in 2018) if John would walk across the Brooklyn Bridge and back. Designed by John A. Roebling four years after the end of the U.S Civil War, the Brooklyn Bridge was the world's first steel-wire suspension bridge. More than a mile long, it rises one hundred thirty-five feet above the surface of the East River. Unlike most bridges, this one's pedestrian walkway is elevated in the center, with the traffic lanes on either side. Gangs that hung out near the bridge made traversing it even more intimidating and treacherous.

A lot of people wouldn't have done it, knowing the Brooklyn Bridge. A long walk, and it wasn't one of your best bridges. He thought I wouldn't do it.

I went at twilight and it took over an hour, round trip. It was scary because of the cars zooming by. The noise effect was chilling. My parents never found out I did it. I wouldn't be alive today if my dad had known.

Around that time John, who had skipped a grade in elementary school, received a scholarship to Bishop Loughlin Memorial High School. That was a big deal in a family as poor as his, but Pasquale had other ideas.

Someone told my dad that the best high school was Brooklyn Prep. It cost $30 a month. Dad told me to turn down the scholarship; he'd find a way to pay the $30. That's how I wound up with a great education from the Jesuits.

At thirteen I was thinking of maybe becoming a priest, because I was an altar boy and all that. There was this priest, Father Collini, who tried to be an influence on me becoming a priest. So I hung with him. He was a great guy.

Brooklyn Prep was a Jesuit-run high school in Crown Heights, just four blocks from Ebbets Field. Its list of notable graduates—in addition to John Parisella, of course—includes former New York University president John Sexton; former U.S. Secretary of Labor Joseph Califano; iconic Penn State football coach Joe Paterno; and lawyer Robert S. Bennett, older brother of former U.S. Secretary of Education William Bennett, who represented, among others, President Bill Clinton in the Monica Lewinsky affair, *New York Times* reporter Judith Miller in the Valerie Plame CIA leak grand jury investigation case, and U. S. Secretary of Defense Caspar Weinberger during the Iran-Contra scandal.

In John's case, he didn't become Rev. Parisella because he just couldn't control his wild side.

At Brooklyn Prep they had what was called the Jug Line. Anytime you did something wrong, you had to walk the Jug Line after school. It was like detention. Instead of sitting an hour after school in a classroom, you actually, literally walked around in a circle where the school was, outside. I was probably on the Jug Line for three and a half of the four years I was there.

> *One of the teachers who put me on the Jug Line—Father Paone, the German teacher—literally hit me with his cane. They were nuts. The one you had to get by, Father Engel—he was like the Prefect—was really tough. He sent me back for a haircut four times. It was too long.*
>
> *One time I had the Racing Form inside of my Latin book, and my Latin teacher, Father Nelson, caught me with it. When he found it, he threw me out. At first he failed me, then they talked to him; I was in the honors program.*

Growing up, John regularly pushed the self-discipline envelope to the breaking point. His father, who had two particularly unruly brothers, once told John's mother: "Two of my kid brothers don't equal how bad your son is."

John started playing the horses as a freshman at Brooklyn Prep. After school he'd catch the A Train to South Ozone Park, home of Aqueduct, or hitch a ride to Belmont, farther away in Elmont. School was over at three o'clock, and the last race finished about five-thirty.

> *My father being a bookmaker, I had knowledge of the racetrack. But my dad didn't want me to bet, so I always placed my bets with bookmakers or at the tracks. He didn't want me to have any part of it.*
>
> *My dad knew I was a gambler since I was a kid. I'd come home for dinner and he'd look at my face. He'd say, "How much did you lose today?" He knew when I lost and when I won, just by my face.*

Pasquale also knew what his son was up to because of his "connections," as illustrated by an episode from John's high school years.

> *I was about 16, playing cards on the street and always winning. My friend comes to me and says, "C'mon, I'll go*

partners with you and I can get you in this card game where we can make some serious money."

So we put up so much apiece. At that time it was a lot of money—maybe a hundred apiece, but a decent-sized bankroll. We went there, and we never won a hand. We lost six hundred. Never won a hand.

So now, my father says to me, "Where were you last Thursday?"

I say, "Whaddya mean? I'm outside, doing different things." He looked at me. "Where were you last Thursday?"

I said, "Okay, I went with my friend to a card game."

He threw six hundred dollars on the table. "Here's your money. Give it to your friend. And if I ever experience this with you again, I'm going to let you get beat and throw you out."

He was giving me an opportunity to be honest. He had already taken care of it because they called him right away. If you had connections, you knew who was scamming and you told people you knew to stay out of certain places.

My friend and I were very humbled. I'm not saying it lasted a long time, but for a while ... Then we thought back on it and reflected on it, and thought how stupid it was that we didn't see it.

That wasn't the only time John and a buddy were shut out playing cards. Again, he was humbled by his dad.

My friend and I, at 16, were the best Pinochle players, so I kept bragging. My father says, "Okay. I'll tell your uncle to come over on Saturday, and you bring your friend." So we played Pinochle for two hours.

My friend and I didn't win one hand—not one hand!

As John's gambling urge grew stronger during his senior year at Brooklyn Prep, he got another taste of his father's family ties.

I got to know this guy that actually sold shoes in a department store. But he was a bookmaker on the side. Once we got to know each other, I told him, "Jeez, I know a lot of people that bet." So he says, "Okay, I'll give you a sheet."

On a sheet, you don't put up money, but you get half back of what the bookmaker's winning. But if the bookmaker loses, you have to make up for that money, first, and then go into the profits.

I didn't really have any clients, so I was doing all the betting. I was stuck twelve thousand dollars, under all different people's names. He found out and went to his people to get the money collected.

Within the Mafia, disputes are often resolved in what is known as a Sitdown. This form of conflict resolution involves a face-to-face meeting in which a person of higher authority listens to both sides in the disagreement and renders a binding decision. It's not unlike arbitration.

My father was close friends with a big figure in the Mafia. So we went to a Sitdown with him.

My dad's friend said, "This is a kid. And you let him run up twelve thousand dollars? You deserve nothing."

The relationship that rescued John from a fixed card game and enabled him to elude the consequences of his deceit with the shoe salesman-bookmaker may help to explain John's later penchant for helping others—even if they didn't always reciprocate or show their appreciation.

Understanding Charlie's Boy

CHARLIE PARISELLA WAS ONE of the few "independents" allowed to operate in mob-controlled enterprises. He went on his own as John was moving on to St. John's University, and became quite successful.

> *My dad had family ties to people who were in the Mafia, but he had no part of that. He distanced himself from the Mafia. Naturally he would socialize with these people, cousins or whatever, but when he was a bookmaker, he basically did it on his own. He didn't want to be locked in.*
>
> *My father was loved by everybody. That's why they let him go—most of the time, you know, they don't let you go. But they loved him. He was full of respect, nothing arrogant. He was just like somebody's best friend.*
>
> *He was a shylock, too, but not one of those 'pay or I'll break your knees' kind. I remember sitting in a restaurant with him at a table, and a guy comes in and says, "I don't have this," and he says, "Alright, bring it in next week."*
>
> *He might have been the only shylock who probably lost money, because he had such a big heart. Nobody would pay him on time.*

Keenly aware of his son's attraction to gambling, Charlie encouraged John to pursue a legitimate career, endorsing his choice of accounting as his major at St. John's. But by then John had been diagnosed with bipolar disorder, a serious emotional illness that goes a long way toward explaining the extremes that became the trademark of his life, and the way he burned through money whenever he had it. "When you are bipolar, you don't think there's going to be a future," he said.

Gambling and substance abuse are two of many so-called manic episodes, or obsessive behaviors, associated with bipolar disorder, which also is known as manic depression. Another of the most common symptoms is extreme mood swings, which many of John's friends experienced with him.

It's estimated that bipolar disorder affects two percent of Americans. Most cases are diagnosed before a person reaches twenty-five years of age, as with John.

I was in therapy at 18, described as manic-depressive. They had, at the time, what they called the Six Months Reserves. I joined that. Then I missed a couple of the meetings, and they sent me to Governor's Island, to the psychiatrist.

My grandfather had died just a few days before, and I was upset. The psychiatrist said, "What's the big deal? He was only a shoemaker." I wanted to hit him with a chair, but the guard there stopped me. I was classified 4F because he said I was nuts.

It was a shock to me, being in a psychiatrist's office at that age. Old-school Italians didn't believe in psychiatrists; the people around me, my family and everyone, thought only crazy people went there.

Charlie avoided involving his son in his day-to-day operations, but did ask John's help on one occasion while he was at St. John's. It resulted in John's rescue from a "bipolar gambling crisis" by another Mafia connection.

> *With my father, I never knew anything about his business. But this one time he asked me to go out to the Island and pick up an envelope for him. It's the only time he ever did, because he never wanted me really to go that deep into what he was doing.*
>
> *I went out there. I was like 19 years old. I was crazy, wild, and a degenerate gambler at the time. I picked up the envelope. It was sealed, but I went ahead and opened it, and there was over eight thousand dollars. So instead of bringing it home to my father, I went to the racetrack.*
>
> *Now, I'm stuck sixty-five hundred. Can't pick a winner where I thought I was the greatest handicapper. And I only have fifteen hundred dollars left. I don't know what to do. I can't make a bet to make up this money. I don't see anything; I'm desperate.*
>
> *As fate would have it, I run into this captain in the Mafia, in the Colombo family, a Wise Guy. We had that connection with the Mafia, but it was a good-time connection*
>
> *He said, "How you doing, John?"*
>
> *"I can't even go home," I told him. He laughed. He said, "What's the matter?" I said, "I blew a lot of my father's money. I'm nuts. I don't know what to do."*
>
> *He says, "Listen, whatever you have left, bet it on Hedley Woodhouse in the last race."*
>
> *I said, "Okay, thanks."*

Hedley Woodhouse was arguably the best jockey ever to come out of Canada, the winner of 2,642 races in his career. He was New York's leading jockey in 1953, and the runner-up on three other occasions.

Hedley Woodhouse's horse has odds that will make me some money. I was desperate, had no picks. I'd blown over six thousand. He gave me a horse that would make me some money. So I did it. I went in twenty minutes before post time and placed my bet, then forgot about it. I said to myself, "I'm a dead man."

Hedley Woodhouse's horse is a closer. In racing terminology, that's a horse that lays sixth, seventh, eighth, and comes off the pace. But in this race, this horse went to the lead!

The race was fixed. I wound up winning almost eleven thousand! To show you how sick I was, I gave my dad his money and went to the trotters that night, and lost the other three thousand.

John would earn a degree in accounting at St. John's, but to coin a variation on a familiar theme: You can take the boy off the streets, but you can't take the streets out of the boy.

St. John's was really just a prelude to going to the racetrack; I'd take classes nine to noon.

I joined an Italian fraternity, Alpha Phi Delta; became pledgemaster then president of the fraternity. There were nineteen of us, and fourteen became doctors, lawyers and dentists.

A very close friend of mine was going to fail; actually two of them. Their marks weren't good enough. One wanted to go to pre-med, and the other wanted to be a dentist. I broke into this teacher's office where they weren't doing good in this class, and I changed their marks, and that's how they got in.

Nah, they didn't discover it. I was too good. I'm from Brooklyn, don't forget.

John entered the business world after graduation, and even taught junior high in Montauk, Long Island for part of a school year. The pay of a teacher was too little, however, and the lure of the track too strong. Eventually he fled New York the way a horse bolts from the barn when the stable door is left open.

I had a job as an auditor at a commercial bank in the city, downtown (Manhattan). I said to my dad, because I was going to the races every day: "I hate this. I want to manage horses. I'm smart enough with my education to put people together and manage horses."

My idea was to put a group together to manage—not to be a horse trainer but to manage—like an owner ... to be in the game. So that's how I initially approached it.

My father, knowing so many people who went broke and lost their apartments, lost this, lost that, didn't want me anywhere near the racetrack. He didn't want me to have any part of the game because he knew I was a gambler from when I was a kid. I had such a bad gambling addiction. I robbed shylock money he would put in the drawer ... I stole his watch—it was incredible.

So what I did was, I left the auditing job and I ran away to Florida.

I was a soda jerk in Florida (making Egg Creams, among other drinks). I also was running an elevator in downtown Miami. I was smoking pot at the time and was stopping at the wrong floors so I got fired on the third day.

I'm in Florida and my father thinks I'm only going to last a few weeks. I was staying with a friend, two of us sleeping on one small bed. After I've been there about six months, my father wanted me to come home because my mother was driving him crazy. She missed her son and just wanted me to come home.

He says, come back and he'll get me a job at the racetrack.

By then, John's lifetime of hobnobbing with celebrities across America had begun—with friends who wore Yankee pinstripes.

Pepi and the Yankees

THE DODGERS LEFT BROOKLYN FOR Los Angeles after the 1957 season, and Ebbets Field was replaced with the largest public housing project in the United States at that time—1,300 apartments in seven 24-story high-rises. Brooklyn baseball fans were understandably disillusioned, angry, confused and, well, just plain lost. "The first betrayal in my life, leading to many," John said some sixty years later. He also said: "I still root against the Dodgers," which is quite a statement considering his youthful allegiance.

Over in the Bronx, meanwhile, the evil Yankees won another American League pennant in 1958, their ninth in eleven years. They would win five more league titles in the next six years, featuring a cast of household names led by Mickey Mantle, Roger Maris and Yogi Berra. In 1961 Maris would hit 61 home runs to break Babe Ruth's single-season record, albeit in eight more games than Ruth played when he set the record in 1927. Maris and Mantle, who slugged 54 homers that year, became the "M&M Boys."

The next season, five years after the Dodgers left Brooklyn, John became a Yankees fan—of sorts—thanks to a rookie named Joe Pepitone, who became one of Mantle's party pals. It marked the beginning of decades of "insider" adventures for John, in many realms.

> *Joe's mother, Angie, went to work for my father in a small restaurant off Atlantic Avenue in Brooklyn. She and my*

mother became close friends, and that's where Joe Pepitone came into the picture.

As a kid growing up in Brooklyn, as a Dodger fan, you were bred to hate the Yankees. So I really had nobody to root for. Then Joe came into my life, and I've been a Yankee fan ever since.

I never went to a Yankee game after the Dodgers left; I hated them.

I finally went to Yankee Stadium because Joe was on the team. My first thought was, "What the hell am I doing here?"

Even though Joe was my friend, one thing doesn't have anything to do with the other. My thoughts were about the Yankees always beating us and calling us bums. That's what I was thinking about.

John's improbable friendship with Joe provided John with experiences others can only dream about.

Because of our mothers' friendship, Joe took a bigger liking to me. It was unbelievable. He took me into the locker room. I went out with them at night. One of the biggest highlights of my career is that I can say I was friends with Mickey Mantle. That was a tremendous highlight.

Pepi, as Joe Pepitone came to be known when he played for the Yankees, was a year older than John and a legendary stickball player in his home neighborhood of Park Slope. It was a working-class, Italian-Irish enclave that produced tough, free-spirited kids; in that way he had a lot in common with John. Joe attended Manual Training High School, which later was renamed John Jay High. While a student there, he was accidentally shot in the stomach by a friend during playground horseplay. Fortunately, the bullet missed all of his vital organs.

Signed as an amateur free agent at the age of 17 (before the institution of the amateur draft), Pepi began his career upstate at Auburn in the Class D New York-Penn League and climbed the minor league ladder during the time John was holding his own in rank-out contests at Louie's, Jug-Lining his way through Brooklyn Prep and playing the horses after school at Aqueduct. After a big season at Amarillo, Pepitone was invited to spring training in 1962, and in typical Pepi fashion, he invited his Brooklyn buddy Parisella to join him in Florida. In equally typical Parisella style, John turned it into a story.

> *We went to Spring Training. I was 19 or something (actually 21) and I did an interview on TV. They saw me around the camp and said, "Are you a prospect." I said, "Yeah, I'm in the farm system." I was like, "Wow!"*
>
> *Pepitone found out and said, "Are you nuts? You'll get me fired."*

On the strength of that big year for Amarillo and a strong performance in Spring Training, Pepi got the call to come to the majors, to the House That Ruth Built—to Yankee Stadium. His first Major League game was April 10, 1962, and on May 5 he hit his first big league homer, a game-winning two-run job that beat the Washington Senators 7-6. He invited John, by then a college guy, into the New York locker room that season, which might seem a brash thing for a rookie to do except that this was Joe Pepitone, the guy who introduced hair dryers in big league clubhouses. Being Pepi's guest gave John a rare look at one of the most famous Yankees of all time.

> *Mickey Mantle loved Joe. That's how I got to be friends with him, because he loved Joe and my connection with Joe. He would tease Joe about being a big sissy with his hair dryer.*

Having Mickey Mantle for a friend, going out with him—and I'm just a college kid!—that was off the charts. I'm a kid from Brooklyn and a friend of Joe Pepitone's; and for Mickey to take me in, put his arm around me while we're out drinking, hanging out and everything ... where does that come from?

Mickey Mantle was an icon. There's nobody today they can say is an icon like him. He was very sincere and warm, very real. In the locker room, he was all class; no antics, not even a joke—serious about the game, big-time.

Mickey was afraid he was going to die at an early age. He would get so drunk we'd literally have to take him home at times.

Mickey would make fun of Pepitone's skinny arms. On the field he'd stop at first base, where Pepitone was, and look over at me in the stands and wave to me and show his muscles. We'd both be laughing. Joe would shrug it off.

John saw almost every Yankee home game during these years, and went out with Pepi, Mantle, Moose Skowron and others once or twice a week. He was a regular in the New York clubhouse, which enabled him to develop first-hand impressions of this generation of Bronx Bombers.

Maris would sit in the corner by himself. No talking. That was him—quiet, in the corner. He was accepted; no dissension or anything. He didn't like the idea of the media drawing comparisons with Mantle. He was very uncomfortable with that. He didn't want any part of that, to be mentioned with Mickey Mantle's name.

Yogi was so simple in nature, and he didn't fit into the crowd. He was an introvert. One time he came up to Joe and said, "How do you spell but? With two Ts?" He was funny, a character. But he wasn't part of the Skowron group. Those guys were wild.

Skowron was nuts! He went out with me and Joe and Mickey all the time.

Bobby Richardson was Bible-oriented, a little on the preacher side.

The manager, Ralph Houk, had that Marine mentality: tough but fair. Players liked him.

The Yankees were so sure they'd found their first baseman of the future in Pepi that they traded nine-year starter Skowron to the Dodgers—the *LOS ANGELES* Dodgers—in November 1962.

Pepi proved to be an able replacement and is ranked among the top 100 all-time Yankees, though below the man called Moose. He hit 27 homers in 1963 and 28 the next season, and drove in 87 then 100 runs as the Yankees won two more American League pennants. (They lost the Series to *those* Dodgers in '63.) Joe was selected to the American League All-Star team both years, and again in 1964. He was heralded as the next Yankee superstar, and even succeeded Mantle in center field when The Mick moved to first base for his last two seasons. But there was too much Brooklyn free spirit in him, as several of his teammates said and John Parisella saw firsthand. An adventure during the 1963 season stands out.

Joe was an incredible athlete. If he had had a work ethic, he would be in the Hall of Fame. He had no work ethic.

One time we partied all night, and fell asleep on the Belt Parkway in Brooklyn. We had to pull off the side of the road. We wake up and it's 9 in the morning, and he says, "I gotta get to the Stadium." We had to rush to the Stadium.

It was a doubleheader that day. The first game he hits a single, a double and a home run; the second game he hits a double his first time up. And this is after we drank all night!

The rest of that story is that Pepi twice was hit by pitches later in that second game, and what has been called the biggest brawl in Yankee Stadium history erupted in the eighth inning after righthander Gary Bell hit him for the second time. Pepi's explanation is vintage Brooklyn childhood. "I was all right until I got to first base," he told reporters after the game. "Then I began calling him names, and he hollered back at me, daring me to come to him. So I did. But I got grabbed from behind. I figured I was going to get hit so I might as well start swinging first."

Dan Topping and Del Webb sold the Yankees to CBS after they lost the 1964 World Series to St. Louis, and a decade of mediocrity followed. Pepitone played for the Yankees through 1969, hitting 166 home runs and compiling an eight-season batting average of .252. He was traded to the Houston Astros that December and sold to the Chicago Cubs in the middle of the 1970 season. The Cubs traded him to Atlanta in May 1973, and the Braves released him a month later to end his major league career. He finished with 219 homers and a .258 career batting average.

An Unlikely Path

IN JOHN'S MEMORY THE LONG TRIP to his first Winner's Circle began in the early 1960s in Saratoga Springs, about two hundred miles from Brooklyn on the southern edge of the Adirondacks, at storied Saratoga Race Course.

The fourth-oldest racetrack in America, classic Saratoga opened for four days of racing a month after the Civil War battles at Gettysburg and Vicksburg, in 1863, and moved across Union Avenue to its long-time location the next year. Set among hundreds of large trees in a pastoral setting that belies the surrounding neighborhood of Victorian mansions, Saratoga competed favorably with genteel Keeneland in Kentucky's Bluegrass Region for overall ambience. (Asked to rank the top paddocks in his career, John responded: "Best experience, to me, was Saratoga. They had the trees outside. Saddling a horse around a tree was something I dreamed about. Incredible memory.")

A popular hangout for celebrities, Saratoga even appeared in the lyrics of the hit song "You're So Vain" by Carly Simon in 1972. The quality of the racing was noteworthy, too, highlighted by the Travers Stakes, considered the "mid-summer Derby" and ranked third among races for three-year-olds behind the first and last legs of racing's Triple Crown.

Saratoga is often called the House of Upsets or Graveyard of Champions for the number of famous horses to lose there. Man-O-War suffered his only loss in the Sanford Stakes in 1919; Triple Crown winner Gallant Fox was beaten by a 100-to-1 longshot in the 1930 Travers Stakes; and the great Secretariat went down to Orion in the Whitney Handicap in 1973. In 2015, Triple Crown winner American Pharoah saw an eight-race winning streak snapped in the Travers by Keen Ice, who didn't win again for twenty-two months.

Opening Day at Saratoga in mid-July each year attracted many women in the kind of hats so common at Churchill Downs on Derby Day—most no doubt from Hatsational, the unique millinery shop downtown. At the same time, the annual throng of twenty to thirty thousand included plenty of folks in shorts lugging coolers and lawn chairs. Before the first post the atmosphere was almost tailgate-like, sans the grills.

John had returned from Florida but Charlie had not yet opened the barn door for him (so to speak) when he approached a veteran horseman outside the racing secretary's office and asked about being a horse trainer.

I went up to one of the leading trainers and said, "I'm looking to be a trainer; what advice can you give me?"

He tells me, "Don't be a trainer."

A couple weeks later I went to him a second time and I said, "I still want to be a trainer."

He says, "I told you, don't be a trainer."

So I ran into him in New York maybe six months later and I said, "Listen. Forget whether or not I want to be a trainer, just give me one of the most important things you experienced knowledge-wise."

He told me to sit in front of that stall for a certain amount of time and observe every part of the horse. And then he walked away.

Becoming a successful Thoroughbred trainer wasn't as natural as it may seem decades later. In fact, this one never rode a racehorse and was fired from his first two stable jobs.

> *I was afraid of horses. We couldn't afford to pay for horseback riding for me, so I was deathly afraid of horses. I couldn't get on a Thoroughbred. Too fast.*

> *It was very difficult at that time because there were no people with money around me or around my dad. So I said, I have to try to be a trainer. This friend said he'd give me an opportunity. It was my father's friend. I worked there one day. I let a horse loose because I was scared, and I got fired.*

> *Then I went on to the next job; still wasn't any good. And I got fired again.*

There's the old saying: "Third time's charm." But of course, there's also the rule: 'Three strikes and you're out." Fortunately for John, the former prevailed—thanks largely to a trainer named Tommy Gullo, who was known as one of the most successful betting trainers of his era (not that John needed any tutelage in that area). Gullo trained horses for forty-five years before his death in 1993 at the age of 69.

> *If Tommy Gullo didn't give me a break, I would never have been a horse trainer. After being fired from my first two jobs in the game—deservedly—I went several months, because who was going to give me a job after that?*

> *A friend of my uncle's had a horse with a trainer at Belmont and explained everything to him. It was Tommy Gullo. He asked Tommy, "As a favor, would you give my friend's nephew a chance?*

> *Tommy told him, "You're being honest with me ...he got fired from two jobs because he's afraid of horses?"*

My uncle's friend said, "Well, Tommy, could you give him a job where his fear of horses wouldn't get in the way? Money's not a factor. He just wants his chance to be around and grow to be comfortable around a horse."

So Tommy gave me a job, just to be in a stall with a horse—forty hours a week, just rubbing a horse's legs with a certain liniment he used. So that was my third job. It was either $30 or $40 a week, seven days a week. All I would do is just rub the legs so I would get accustomed to being around a horse. I couldn't walk a horse because I was afraid.

From there I took all the steps up the ladder: hot-walker, then a groom, then assistant trainer. Those were the steps. Two years with him, seven days a week, working nine to ten hours a day. I wouldn't have been in the game if it hadn't been for him.

Ken Dunn interacted with John through decades in management at Hollywood Park, Atlantic City, Fair Grounds, Arlington and in Florida, where Dunn was president of Calder from 1990 to 1999 then senior vice president of Florida Operations for Churchill Downs Inc. until 2008. He didn't know about the advice John got at Saratoga, but years later he saw it in action many times. "When I picture John as a horse trainer," Dunn said, "I can see him sitting on a stool in front of a stall. Whether it was a horse with a problem or one of his favorites, he would sit there for hours, watching them in the stall."

I learned so much. It would take more than one day, but their mannerisms in the stall, how they're feeling ... if they're on the upgrade, or the downgrade ... where they are at that point psychologically.

A horse is very true to what work is put into them.

John became a close friend of Tommy Gullo's son, Gary, who started working in his father's barn when he was fourteen and later became a trainer of note in his own right. "I was seven, eight, years old," Gary said. "My father had John tutor me and my brother because he went to college and was very smart. We were screwing around in school. My dad said to John, 'Just make sure they learn what they're supposed to learn.'"

So John became the tutor of Tommy's boys, but it didn't quite work out the way Tommy intended. "With John we didn't study or anything," Gary Gullo said. "We had some pillow fights and just played around. I tease John about it: 'If you would have taught me something, I could have been something. I could have been a doctor or a lawyer or something.'

"He's kind of like a brother to me. Once I got training on my own, I would definitely ask him what to do with certain horses. I would ask him for advice on a lot of things, whether it was people in general, owners, jockeys, horses. Anytime I needed advice, I would ask him. To me he is one of the best horse trainers around."

Campo's Protégé

EVERY THOROUGHBRED TRAINER POINTS to another trainer as his or her mentor. In John Parisella's case, that trainer was John Campo.

Another Italian New Yorker, who grew up near Aqueduct (in South Ozone Park, Queens, rather than John's Brooklyn), Campo saddled more than 1,400 winners in a 28-year career. Besides John, he mentored several other eventual trainers of note, including Hall of Famer Nick Zito, who won the Kentucky Derby twice, and Pete Ferriola, Mitch Friedman and Bruce Levine. Growing up, he was a fan of the television cowboy-singer Roy Rogers, and once saved enough money to buy a palomino that looked like Rogers' famous horse Trigger. He worked for famed trainer Eddie Neloy for nine years, starting as a stable hand.

Actor Jack Klugman, who at one time hired Parisella to train his horses and gave him the "Trainer to the Stars" title, once said of the colorful Campo: "He's by Damon Runyon out of a Don Rickles mare." That was Klugman's glib way of capturing the brash personality of Parisella's rotund, cigar-chomping mentor, who, after winning the 1981 Kentucky Derby with Pleasant Colony, told respected ABC-TV sportscaster Jim McKay: "He won because I'm a good horse trainer, pal, and don't ever forget it." (That was AFTER Neloy told him to take a Dale Carnegie course so he'd complement his obvious training talent with a more polished approach with people.)

> *My next step was with one of the best trainers ever in the game, John Campo. Tommy Gullo was very sick so his horses were cut back. As fate turned out, Campo's barn was right*

next to his. I was friendly with Campo because he was such a big winner. I always asked him a lot of questions.

He saw that I put all the hours in; even though I was afraid of horses, I rubbed their legs for hours. For some reason, he liked me. He knew I was out of work so he gave me a job.

My job there was to be assistant trainer, which was a big leap, especially to be with him because he was the number-one trainer in New York. I spent two-and-a-half years with him, seven days a week, twelve to fourteen hours a day. It was only because of him that I accomplished what I did in my career, from having him as a teacher and the work ethic of seven days a week, fourteen hours a day. That's where I was sleeping with the horse.

I remember asking him for a day off, and he said, "Sure, take three or four. You see how many days I take off." Which he never took a day off. So I made sure I was there an hour early the next day because I didn't want to jeopardize myself by asking for a day off. I didn't want to show him I was soft.

I went with a horse with him to Jersey to run a big stakes race, and he said, "You stay with this horse all night." I sat on a bucket and I stayed there all night, never left. I had to make sure the muzzle stayed and all that. I loved it.

And just as Neloy eventually pushed Campo out of his stable and told him it was time to fly on his own, Campo did that to Parisella.

It was incredible how much I learned there. I didn't want to leave him, but one time he wasn't there and I took something on my own, that he taught me, with a horse at Saratoga. I took it upon myself, which I had no right doing, and the horse won. He came up the next day and he fired me. He didn't really fire me, but he said, "You know what? Forget this. It's time for you to go on your own."

It wasn't so much firing, because he was very fond of me. It was two things: That I was ready, and that he was a great teacher, and just like in sports, you don't do something unless the coach tells you to do it.

To show he was right, that I was ready to go on my own, I was fifth-leading trainer my first year in New York. And I don't know anything! If I don't have Campo during that year, no way. It took me three or four years for me to be able to tell you I was knowledgeable and decent at what I was doing.

Even though John was on his own by mid-1969, his relationship with his mentor remained strong for decades.

I followed Campo, everything he did. I ran to him with every problem. I remember one time I had a horse break out in hives. I never saw that in my five years! I ran to him, scared to death, and he said, "Don't scratch him. It was probably a bee sting or something like that."

That horse, a cheap horse, wound up finishing fourth in the Metropolitan, one of the biggest races of the year.

Campo's protégé had been on his own for more than a decade when Campo took Pleasant Colony to Churchill Downs for the 1981 Kentucky Derby. John watched from the grandstand as Pleasant Colony held off a finishing drive by Woodchopper to win by three-quarters of a length. Then he helped load the dark bay three-year-old for the trip to the second leg of racing's Triple Crown, the Preakness Stakes at Pimlico, where Pleasant Colony came from behind to beat Bold Ego by a length.

Campo was one race away from winning racing's biggest prize, but his protégé detected a problem.

The only time he didn't listen to me was going into the Belmont, when Pleasant Colony was going for the Triple Crown. When I heard the jockey, (Jorge) Velasquez, was meditating, I said, "We have no shot."

So I go in the office and I close the door. And I say, "John. Velasquez says he's meditating. Jockeys don't have the mentality to meditate! This guy's meditating! We're dead. Please, you gotta take him off this horse."

He said, "Are you crazy?" He couldn't envision what I was saying to him. He thought I was off the charts. He kept Velasquez, and Pleasant Colony finished third to Summing.

By then, John Parisella had made "the big time"—"the ONLY trainer to ever have a full story with a photo in *The New York Times*," he said—and had experienced the calamity of a barn fire that nearly wiped him out. In one of those tragedies that define irony, his mentor would go through the same thing five years after missing out on the Triple Crown, losing thirty-six of thirty-eight stabled in a barn at Belmont Park.

Photo Finish

NINETEEN SIXTY-NINE WAS A historic year—for America, for New York City sports fans, and for John Parisella. Its twelve months are captured well in memorable quotes:

> "That's one small step for man, one giant leap for mankind," Neil Armstrong famously proclaimed as he stepped onto the surface of the moon.

> "Hey, I got news for you. We're going to win Sunday, I'll guarantee you," Broadway Joe Namath boldly promised in response to a heckler at a dinner honoring him in Miami a few days before Super Bowl III.

> "We cannot learn from one another until we stop shouting at one another," newly elected President Richard M. Nixon told America, then torn by anti-Vietnam War protests, in his first inaugural address.

> "I don't hit the ball when I need to. I can't steal when I need to. I can't score from second when I need to. I can't play anymore," Mickey Mantle sadly admitted in announcing his retirement as spring training began.

> "Woodstock was a thing of beauty," singer Joni Mitchell crooned of the gigantic music festival in Bethel, New York that attracted more than four hundred thousand mostly young fans of more than thirty rock groups.

> "Dammit, we can beat these guys," a teammate of star pitcher Tom Seaver is said to have shouted in the Miracle Mets locker room after the Mets lost the first game of the World Series to heavily favored Baltimore.

And,

> "I'm not telling them we lost, but I'm not saying we won, either," John recalled of the day he broke his maiden as a trainer.

Yes, it was the year America finally reached the moon and Richard Nixon assumed the U.S. Presidency; when the Jets became the first American Football League team to win a Super Bowl, making Joe Namath's prediction come true with a 16-7 upset of the Baltimore Colts; when the Mantle era ended and the Miracle Mets became the first expansion team to win a World Series, upsetting the heavily favored Baltimore Orioles four games to one to cap their first winning season in team history. (Also in 1969, the New York Knicks began a season that culminated in an NBA championship the following May, when Willis Reed ignored a torn thigh muscle to inspire his Knicks to a seventh-game victory over the Los Angeles Lakers.)

As dramatic and memorable as those events were, they don't top that suspenseful day when Colonel Bay reached the Winner's Circle at Monmouth Park in Oceanport, New Jersey. At least not in the life and career of John Parisella. For any trainer, there's nothing like that first victory. Almost fifty years later, John recalled the moment—including sweating the outcome—as if he were reliving it hours after the race.

> *My father put four friends together and the five people put up five hundred apiece because my father had no money to back me. The five of them plus five other guys—and there are affiliations there—were all waiting for the winner to be posted. It was a photo finish.*

> *The photo was like fifteen minutes. A couple of my dad's cousins were in the Mafia and they had bet big money.*
>
> *I'm not telling them we lost, but I'm not saying we won, either.*
>
> *Can you imagine if they had put up the other horse? We won by less than a nose.*

Charlie Parasella did more than just get his son started as a trainer back in 1969. He also kept Mafia elements from influencing John in any way.

> *My dad made sure when I became a trainer—he let them all know: "I don't want any discussions with my son about race horses. He'll say hello to you; he'll acknowledge you and give you that respect. But that's it. I don't want to hear anything about him giving you a loser or anything like that."*
>
> *He had the higher-up people behind him; his cousins were very strong, well up in the Mafia, so he was able to accomplish that. So I was never, ever, involved. He was well-loved and respected. There was no problem.*

* * *

JOHN ENJOYED ALMOST IMMEDIATE SUCCESS, sparking a story in *The New York Times* in 1971 that recognized him as "an up-and-comer." In it he noted how the way he was treated by others on the backside at Belmont had changed as he experienced greater success.

> "It's unreal, the things that go on here," John was quoted. "It's a game of envy, jealousy, scheming—insecure people trying to make themselves secure by knocking the other guy, undermining him. The more successful you become, the more you get knocked.
>
> "One day a guy's your best friend; the next day he doesn't want to talk to you.

"When I had three cheap horses, I was the greatest guy in the world. It was always, 'Hey Johnny, how you doing?' Then things got better, and it started...

"Listen, I don't want to sound like an ingrate," he also said. "I'm only 28. I'm grateful for the chance I got. But the racetrack is like a perpetual elevator—everything going up or down all the time. It's got to be the most competitive business in the world, tougher than the stock market, tougher than the real estate game."

That story also acknowledged John's first notable reclamation project, that "cheap horse" that had a case of hives when John consulted with Campo. The six-year-old named Here Comes Trouble had had multiple surgeries for leg fractures, and most horsemen saw only the "trouble" part. But John saw something else. He claimed him for $5,000.

I spent 4-5 hours a day with him. At the time I could do that since I only had three horses in my barn.

He went up the ladder, going from claiming races to allowances then finishing fourth in The Metropolitan Mile, at the time one of the premier stake races in the United States.

One day I had to attend a meeting in the City, and while leaving, by chance, I get on the elevator with Sigmund Sommer, a New York real estate tycoon and number one horse owner at the time. We were both on our way to Aqueduct Racetrack for the feature race of the day.

I was running Here Comes Trouble and he had the 3-5 favorite in the race, named Feathered Rule. He says to me, "Son, don't feel bad. You will finish a strong second because I have a much better horse . . you don't have a chance."

> *I didn't respond immediately but as we were leaving the building my parting words were, "I hope you are not a crybaby, but you will get beat today...I promise."*
>
> *Here Comes Trouble beats him easily.*
>
> *Sommer didn't congratulate me, but I got used to that kind of treatment since I was an outsider from Brooklyn without a real horse racing background.*

John's early career took a detour on June 8, 1972 when thirty-seven Thoroughbreds perished in a horrific blaze at Bostwick Stables in Westbury, Long Island. Half of them were being trained by John.

A newspaper story reported that the fire was discovered around 3 a.m. by a groom, who said he tried to open the barn door with the assistance of a police officer but was driven away by the intense heat. One report said the fire was fed by two tons of recently delivered hay. John had to defend himself legally while mourning the loss of his horses.

> *Another trainer told me at 5:30 in the morning. All my horses were destroyed.*
>
> *It was devastating to me. When I heard, I didn't even go to work. I went home. I didn't know what to do with myself. I love all animals; they were a part of my life.*
>
> *The farm sued me. They tried to say I was responsible for the fire, when I wasn't even there. I had nothing to do with it.*
>
> *It went to court. The way my attorney handled it the first day—forget about it. He didn't have any knowledge of defense regarding the death of these horses. I fired him after one day and defended myself.*
>
> *I explained I wasn't there; that it was a big loss to my career;*

that it cost me all kinds of money. But I didn't care about that. I cared about losing my animals. It took me one day, and they cleared me of responsibility the next day.

John doesn't blame the late Ken Noe Jr. for the fire, and in fact speaks well of him. But he does feel Noe treated him poorly back then and holds him somewhat responsible. Noe had been named racing secretary and handicapper for the NYRA that year, and it was because of Noe that John's horses wound up where they were when the fire broke out.

We had a problem because he had two real good friends, and I was tied with one of them for the championship of the meet that was going on then at Belmont. So he cut my stall space to make sure his friend won. I had to put a bunch of my horses on a farm about fifteen or twenty minutes from Belmont and bring them to the track when they ran.

He was someone I really respected, because he loved the game and wanted to make sure it was played in a fair way, and that whatever stall space was given, those people deserved the space they got. I was on the wild side, and that's the complete opposite—the antithesis—of what he was.

Eventful months awaited. With his flamboyant, engaging personality in full bloom, John would go to California to put personal losses behind him, be a repeat guest on national television and become part of the hip Hollywood scene.

First Turn

Previous page: Bethenny enjoying a childhood Christmas; Bethenny with her mom, John and Msgr. Edward Melton when John arranged a private baptism and First Communion for her; John, Bethenny, "Bonnie" and her mother on Bethenny's 12th birthday *(photos courtesy of Bernadette Birk)*

'Trainer to the Stars'

THE LATE CAUSTIC COMEDIAN DON RICKLES, who made a hugely successful career out of insulting people, once described his manager, Joe Scandore, as "a man with connections"—you know, the kind that meant the difference between being a headliner and a warm-up act in the entertainment world of the Thirties and Forties. When Scandore died in 1986, said Rickles, those "connections" showed up at the church and the cemetery in Lincolns and Cadillacs.

Joe Scandore was commonly referred to as John Parisella's uncle, even though he wasn't actually a blood relative. He and Pasquale Parisella were such good friends they pledged to look after each other's son if either of them died or was unable. That made Scandore John's Italian uncle. Uncle Joe was significant in the early part of John's life and career as a horse trainer, though not because of his "connections."

> After getting fired twice, I went to live with my uncle. I was down, depressed. I didn't know what to do with my life. Wherever he went, he took me. I made like twenty to twenty-five trips with my uncle to places where Rickles was performing—many times to Las Vegas.
>
> There would be times where they'd have differences of opinion, and Rickles would refer to me and say, "Would you tell your uncle he's nuts."

He definitely broke my uncle's balls. He was a pain in the ass many times. But he wasn't as bad as his appearance. That was his schtick.

Scandore was there for John, too, after that devastating barn fire in Westbury and, as they had pledged, following Pasquale's death to cancer that summer. Eventually he would introduce him to the world of Hollywood, which led to many celebrity experiences including friendships with singers Paul Anka, Neil Diamond and Frankie Valli, and composer Burt Bacharach and his actress wife Angie Dickinson.

I still had eight horses on the track. I stayed in New York for a while, then went to California. I stayed at my uncle's hacienda.

When I first went there, I was so upset I didn't want any part of horse racing. For six weeks I wanted to become involved in disco music professionally, to follow in my uncle's footsteps. I went around with my uncle.

After returning to the sport he loved and making it as a trainer, John found himself on national television, talking horse racing on "The Tonight Show Starring Johnny Carson." It was April 1973, and in the weeks to come the incomparable Secretariat would become the first horse to win the Triple Crown in twenty-five years. (John, though, picked another horse to win The Kentucky Derby that night because, "I didn't want to pick against one of the other trainers in the race.") Engaging, colorful and a rising star among trainers, John was the perfect guest for the subject.

He made a second appearance later with Hollywood celebrities James Caan and Jack Klugman, and that night Klugman christened him the "Trainer to the Stars." The sobriquet fit by then because Klugman *(Quincy M.D.)*, Telly Savalas *(Kojak)*, Don Adams *(Get Smart)* and Caan—introduced to John by Scandore and Rickles—had all hired John to train their horses, and several other celebrities had become his friends.

Johnny Carson, of course, had a name of his own: "The King of Late Night."

And King he was.

Before there was a Jimmy Fallon, a Jimmy Kimmel, a Stephen Colbert or a Seth Meyers—before Leno or Letterman—there was Ed McMahon, to the accompaniment of Skitch Henderson's studio band, intoning nightly: "... *Heeeeere's Johnny*..." From October 1, 1962 through May 22, 1992—thirty years and 4,531 shows!—Johnny Carson dominated late-night network TV, his audience measured in the millions. In 2002 his "The Tonight Show Starring Johnny Carson" was ranked twelfth in *TV Guide's* "50 Greatest TV Shows of All Time." Carson received six Emmy Awards and the 1985 Peabody Award for excellence in broadcasting, and was inducted into the Television Academy Hall of Fame. In 1992 he was awarded the Presidential Medal of Freedom.

It was Johnny's show even when he had a guest host, which happened often and was the case both times that John appeared. Filling the chair behind Johnny's desk those nights was Rickles, who had monikers of his own: "Mr. Warmth" and "The Merchant of Venom" among them. Also dubbed "Comedy's Equal Opportunity Offender," Rickles appeared for the first time on Carson's show in 1965, and encored more than a hundred times. It was he who invited John.

There is a similarity of purpose, if nothing else, between a horse track's paddock, which John frequented for decades, and a television Green Room, in which John found himself not only for his Carson appearances but also when the "Dean Martin Celebrity Roast," a hit television show at the time, roasted the host.

A paddock is where a horse trainer soothes and saddles his Thoroughbred—a unique and often high-strung personality—before sending it to the post parade, the starting gate and, inevitably, the race. In the paddock, the trainer takes care of his client, the horse's owner, too, reassuring him or her and making them feel at ease and important. ("You want to perform," John says. "There's pressure. It's something special, a great feeling.")

In a Green Room, personalities of a different sort—a show's guests—try to relax, finish prepping, and bide their time until they go before the cameras and engage with the host. It's the final stop after makeup, the last place to calm the nerves—if they need calming, as John, to his surprise, found is sometimes the case. His night at the Dean Martin Roast was particularly adventurous.

> *It's funny. You would never think it, but Howard Cosell was a nervous wreck. You'd never think it, knowing him, but he was. We talked about what was going on that year in sports.*
>
> *I was in the Green Room with Joe Namath—and Ali, too. He spoke very little. Lee Marvin was nuts. I remember him grabbing my leg. He said, "Don't make a move."*
>
> *I was in makeup next to Jimmy Stewart. He was a quiet, classy man. I had a respectful conversation with him. He wasn't very outgoing. I'm saying to myself, "I don't belong here." I guess that's why I wasn't nervous.*
>
> *I spoke only two or three minutes with Hubert Humphrey because he was the typical politician. I spoke for about an hour with Barry Goldwater. What a sincere, wonderful individual. I checked with a few other people, and they confirmed what I felt.*
>
> *We talked about his thoughts and his theories, about being aggressive, not passive. He was interested in horse racing because he knew nothing about it.*

Riding red-eye flights during most of 1973, John commuted between New York and California, training and running horses in both states. He won 19.4% of the races he entered (finishing first eighty-six times—second highest yearly total of his career), and at one point saddled eight straight winners, a New York record for consecutive wins.

* * *

IT'S BEEN WRITTEN MANY TIMES that John trained horses for Rickles. But, John said, the searing insult specialist wasn't the type to have horses. "Too cheap."

However, John once trained a horse that was *named* Don Rickles. It was John's idea. "My uncle went to him and he loved it."

Don Rickles, the horse, won his first maiden race August 4, 1983 at Saratoga then, seventeen days later, placed (ahead of eventual Kentucky Derby and Belmont winner Swale) in the Hopeful Stakes, the first stakes race for East Coast two-year-olds, also at Saratoga. In his third start, at Aqueduct that November, "he broke sideways and was eliminated at the start," John told a writer. But nineteen days later Don Rickles won the Nashua Stakes at Aqueduct. In three years he won four of eighteen starts, but Don Rickles the comedian was unmoved.

"I was hoping he'd buy a horse or two," John said. "It didn't work."

John's connection to Rickles through his "uncle" opened the door to business relationships with actors Klugman, Savalas, Adams and Caan, and friendships with Burt Reynolds and other entertainers. They all were drawn to what John often termed his "wild" side—his outgoing, fun-loving, risk-taking personality.

He became particularly close to Caan, whose career took off after he played terminally ill Chicago Bears running back Brian Piccolo in the 1971 television movie *Brian's Song*, then hot-tempered Sonny Corleone in the Oscar-winning film *The Godfather* a year later. In 1974 Caan received a two-year-old named Cowboy Obsession as a gift and quickly became obsessed himself with horse racing. He gave John $50,000 and told him to put together a stable. The next year Caan's horses cashed eight purse money checks in ten starts early in the meeting at Aqueduct—enough to merit a story in *The New York Times*.

John noted that Caan had been pictured in *The Daily Racing Form* and that the movie star had told John he was making him famous. At Aqueduct a few weeks earlier, John said, two girls fainted when Caan showed up. He said he had fan mail—a couple hundred letters—piling up at the barn.

John lived with Caan and *M*A*S*H* star Elliot Gould at Caan's home in Beverly Hills for a time while he was in California, and that exposed John to the world of Hollywood moviemaking.

The sequel to *Funny Girl*—*Funny Lady*—starred Caan, who was thirty-four, opposite thirty-two-year-old Barbra Streisand (whose eight-year marriage to Gould had ended in divorce in July 1971). Commenting on the selection of Caan as the film's male lead over Robert Blake, Robert DeNiro and Al Pacino, Streisand is quoted as saying: "It comes down to whom the audience wants me to kiss. Robert Blake? No. James Caan? Yes."

> *I had a pass from Day One. I could have gone every day. I went maybe the third day. I said, "Wow. This will be great, to see a movie made." It was so boring I never went back.*

John did use the pass, though, to deliver cocaine to Caan, who years later spoke openly about his habit. "I went through it," he is quoted saying in a 1991 newspaper story, "but not to the degree you've heard about. I wish I had done half the things people said I did."

> *He needed some energy as a wakeup call from the night before. I was running cocaine over to the trailer where he would use that to help him get through the day.*

The end of filming in July 1974 provided John with a lasting memory.

> *I found out from Jimmy that it was custom for the two top*

stars to exchange gifts. Jimmy comes running like a madman into the house and says, "Would you believe this? I spent two thousand dollars getting her a gift, and look at this thing. It's not worth fifty dollars."

Living with Caan also led to an unforgettable evening with Barbi Benton at the Playboy Mansion. Benton lived there with Playboy founder Hugh Hefner for seven years in the 1970s and is known for discovering what became known as Playboy Mansion West. Located near Los Angeles Country Club and the UCLA campus, the mansion sat on 5.3 acres, had twenty-nine rooms, and measured almost 22,000 square feet. It was about as far from the streets of Brooklyn as John could have gotten the night Caan invited him to join him there.

He said, "Why don't you go over with me? I've been there before. You'll love it there."

We drove in, and the mansion was incredible. It had this game room that had like twelve different pinball machines; regular-sized theater—anything you wanted. It was a big party—Francis Ford Coppola and a lot of great people were there.

Hefner's No. 1 girl was Barbi Benton. We got to meet going through the mansion, and somehow we hit it off, talking. So we went for a walk. He had woods and everything. We didn't realize the time, but we wound up talking for three hours.

It was like she was never really around real people, because of her lifestyle, and I was so down-to-earth and a street guy and all that. She found that fascinating. We talked about everything. She was a sweetheart.

Benton was the subject of four covers and several nude photo layouts in Playboy (though never a Playmate of the Month centerfold). Her relationship with Hefner began while she was still a teenager when Hefner, who was then 42, asked her for a date. "I don't know; I've never dated anyone over 24 before," she reportedly said, to which Hefner reportedly replied: "Neither have I."

> *Hefner ran to Jimmy and said, "Where's your friend? I can't find Barbi, and she's with him."*
>
> *As we're coming back, Jimmy Caan comes at me, screaming: "Where the heck were you? Are you crazy? You gotta get off the grounds right now."*
>
> *You had to see Jimmy. He says, "You're barred from going to the Playboy Mansion. Are you crazy? You disappear with Barbi Benton? You almost got me barred."*

Following in Caan's racing tracks, Savalas, Klugman and Adams became partners in Our Thing Stable in 1975 and gave John $150,000 to claim or buy stock for the Hollywood Park meeting that April. "They call me their genius," he told a writer then. "They're giving me free rein." He trained for them for about four years and, in retrospect, said, "In the racing game they did great—they broke even."

Hollywood Park and Santa Anita were fierce competitors in the 1970s and early 1980s, and Marjorie (Marje) Everett, part-owner and chief executive officer of Hollywood Park, was as shrewd an operator as John was a flamboyant trainer. Marje enforced a strict dress code in the Turf Club at Hollywood Park, and it was virtually inevitable that John would run afoul of it. Ken Dunn was assistant general manager there at this time, the Turf Club one of his responsibilities.

"John was on one of his many highs, in between his almost-as-many lows, training for James Caan," Dunn recalled. "California was very liberal—long hair, flowered silk shirts and bell-bottom pants. If you wanted to go into the Turf Club, you had to have a coat and tie on. Eventually the coat and tie was relaxed to leisure suit and a silk shirt, but you still had to put a tie on. Or an ascot.

"So John shows up in the Turf Club. He's got a coat and tie on, but no socks, and sneaks. I had to let him in. I said, 'John, what are you doing to me? I gotta let you in, but don't do this again. Please put shoes and socks on.'"

> *I wasn't trying to make a statement. During that time—and it was very warm—I had a tendency to not wear socks for many years in my life. So, without thinking about it, I went in there without socks and they wouldn't let me in.*
>
> *I said to them, I know you don't have socks for me to wear, but I really don't want to go all the way home and miss the races. So I called Ken, and he tells them to let me in.*

* * *

Having already been acclaimed "Trainer to the Stars" by then, John also had started down the road that eventually led to another title: "Stepfather to a Star." It had started innocently sometime in 1970, getting to know a woman he would call Bonnie. She was the estranged wife of fellow trainer and friend Bobby Frankel, who was the mother of a little girl named Bethenny.

John's 'Bonnie'

BORN IN BROOKLYN FOURTEEN MONTHS before John, Robert Frankel saddled his first winner three years ahead of John: Double Dash at Aqueduct in November 1966. It was the start of a Hall of Fame career that saw Frankel win 3,654 races in 17,657 starts—a .207 winning percentage. He received the Eclipse Award for best trainer six times, and won the Pacific Classic Stakes a record six times, including four years in a row. In 2003 he won the Belmont Stakes with Empire Maker.

Frankel was a lot like John, without the flamboyant personality: brash, street-smart, and a pretty successful gambler at an early age. And just as John hit it off with a sports legend in Rick Pitino, Frankel clicked with a member of the Baseball Hall of Fame, former Yankees manager Joe Torre, who bought his first Thoroughbred in partnership with Frankel. In 2005 they won the Queen's Plate, first leg of the Canadian Triple Crown, with Wild Desert.

John and Frankel developed a professional friendship—Frankel paid John for every claim he recommended, and even offered him an opportunity to train some of Frankel's horses at Monmouth Park at triple what John was making with Tommy Gullo. But that never came to be.

> *It was a great opportunity to go on my own. But one of my codes was loyalty, so I turned it down because Gullo was sick and I was taking care of his barn for him.*

The friendship disintegrated in part because of differences at the racetrack and partly because of Frankel's failed marriage to Bernadette

Birk—mother of Bethenny Frankel (Yes, THAT Bethenny Frankel)—and her and John's eventual marriage. Ironically, in John's first race in California, at Santa Anita, he entered a 20-to-1 longshot in a race in which Bobby Frankel saddled the favorite, and they finished in a dead heat.

> *Bobby Frankel and I had been friendly; you know, trainers standing at the rail rooting for each other's horses. There was a lot of animosity between us after that.*

Called Bobby by many even though he disliked it, Frankel married Bernadette around the time John won his first race. She was not yet nineteen, wrote THAT Bethenny Frankel in one of her books, portraying her mother as petite, blond-haired and green-eyed. Bernadette was the daughter of a horse trainer, and thus familiar with the backside at racetracks. In the book, Bethenny characterized her mother with many of the words used to describe herself: smart, sassy, talented, sarcastic, ballsy, opinionated and a fighter. Bethenny was born on her mother's twentieth birthday, in November 1970.

In early 1971 Bethenny's father went to California and enjoyed some success at Santa Anita. "Naturally, I and my baby went with him," Bernadette said. The next year he made California his base, setting the Hollywood Park spring meeting record with sixty winners. But California was not a full-time home for his wife. "Every couple months I would go back to New York with my daughter, for various reasons," Bernadette said, "because we had two residences, California and New York."

Frankel has been described as "focused before that term became fashionable." Such single-mindedness was good on the backside and the track but not so much at home, where his possessiveness restricted his wife in ways she ultimately could not accept.

"Bobby wouldn't allow me to go to school or to go to work," recalled Bernadette, who later became a highly regarded interior "architectural" designer—the only woman working in a firm with several men when she began—and later went on to teach at four colleges in New York City. "I was supposed to go back to New York to go to school. He said, 'You're not going to school.'"

"He wouldn't allow me to do anything," she continued. "When he would go out with friends, you know, like guys do, to basketball games and stuff like that, I had to go with him. I'm not saying he treated me badly. In fact, he was very good and generous to me. He just wanted me to be like the other wives—hair, nails, clothes etc., all of which I found boring and inconsequential. It's just that he was cold like a robot."

According to Bethenny, writing in one of her books, Bobby refused to return to New York because the owner for whom he was training in California told him he'd find another trainer if Bobby left. That was the beginning of the end. Eventually Bernadette moved back to New York for good, and she and Bobby divorced.

John and Bernadette had met in the owners' dining room at Belmont in early 1970.

There's a room at the track they call the Trustees Room, which is a special room you go to when you have special people, or for big races. I had my run of New York so I could walk in there anytime.

"My husband's owner had this same huge table on weekends," Bernadette said, "and John showed up at that table. I thought he was at the wrong table, but somebody had told him to sit at that table."

I trained horses for a stockbroker who worked for Willie Frankel, who was Bobby Frankel's number-one client (same last name, no relation) in New York. We went to lunch a few times, and that's how I met Bonnie. Her sister Tory worked on the track. I was very friendly with her sister.

"I was going to England," Bernadette continued, "and there was a book he needed that you supposedly could only get in London at a particular bookshop. We spent the whole lunch talking just like as friends. We never dated for almost two years."

Bernadette went abroad, came back with the book for John, and thought no more about him. "I did not see John in California at all," she emphasized.

Bernadette became Bonnie ("My name is not Bonnie; it's Bernadette. That was John's nickname for me.") when John started seeing her regularly in the summer of 1972. ("I'm a nickname guy, just like Clipboard, Eggplant and them. I didn't want to go through any Bernadette shit.")

"Bonnie" described the start of their relationship this way:

"I knew him as a friend from the racetrack. His father was dying, the second year, of lung cancer, and he couldn't deal with it. I had a very large apartment so he would stay at my apartment so as to not face his dying father all the time. (Pasquale was only fifty-three when cancer finally claimed him in August 1972.)

"We were not intimate in any way whatsoever," Bernadette said. "We were merely friends. At the same time, I saw how he adored my daughter and treated her. He was, from the beginning, devoted to her. After two years of being friends, we went on a date."

I got to spend time with Bonnie and her sister Tory, hanging out at Bonnie's apartment. She had left her husband in California. They separated. She was by herself in the apartment in Queens with Bethenny

My father had died—in my arms—and I needed to get out of the house. I was in a bad place.

Bonnie was asking Tory if she could look after Bethenny while she finished her last year of design school. Tory couldn't, with her hours.

I didn't have a high profile then; I had like eight horses. So I offered. I said, "Look, my mom's got people (to be with her). Even when you want to go somewhere at night, I'll look after Bethenny. It'll give me a chance to not sleep in my house."

I had no bad habits at the time, like drugs, plus I was good friends with her sister.

Bethenny was a terror. You know, the terrible twos. Her grandparents couldn't handle her ... her mother and father were apart ...her mother was in school. Bethenny was tough.

For one year it was just a friendship, and Bethenny and me bonding since we were spending so much time together. Her mom was going to school. She had a life separated from her husband, going into the City on the weekends.

I had no concern whatsoever of going anywhere since my father passed away. It was good therapy for me. During that year, I would go to the City with her and her sister, and it was nothing. It was great having a place to remove myself. After a year we started feeling something for each other.

Bonnie made me believe how intelligent I was. I really didn't believe it, being somebody coming from the streets. She gave me that confidence. She played a big role in my life.

When we started caring for each other, Bethenny was already a part of my life. We got married six months or a year later.

The way Bernadette tells it, the wedding was a surrender of sorts. "He was a very, very nice man, and he adored my daughter," she said. "That was number one: He adored my daughter. He kept asking me for well over a year, as did his mother. So I really got sick of saying no. He's basically a very good person, a naturally good person. I respected him; I cared for him. But the number one reason was he adored my daughter, and she was number one in my life."

Bernadette described a family life that, despite other dysfunctions, was surprisingly typical in some ways.

"I got John interested in old movies from the Thirties and Forties," Bernadette said. John's favorite actor was Humphrey Bogart, and his favorite movie, Casablanca. He particularly liked love stories. "I would spend hours watching them," she continued, "and he got into it but not to my extent. We really had films, in general, in common and enjoyed our time together. We would have film marathon days, going from film to film at the local multiplex.

"We would go over to John's grandmother's house in Brooklyn for the large, traditional Italian Sunday dinners and card games with all the relatives," she said. "There was so much food: eggplant Parmesan, vegetables, baked ziti and lasagna. His grandmother spoke practically no English; she would say to me 'manga, manga'—eat, eat. She would send me to nap after the meal, while the other women had to clean up. I guess they didn't appreciate that.

"Bethenny would look forward to going there and play with John's nieces."

The way Bernadette dealt with John's rough street talk is another example.

"I was raised by my mother, a British woman who expected perfect manners and, of course, no public display of emotions," she said. "John would use the "F" word at least five times a paragraph. It was very offensive to me, and I did not want Bethenny exposed to that language. I got him out of that habit by tapping him on the shoulder or hand every time he used the "F" word. It took a pretty long time, but it worked."

> *I was a kid from Brooklyn, and she really helped refine me.*
> *I was like a diamond in the rough, and she brought that out*
> *of me.*

Bernadette recalled other examples of the good side of life with John.

"John knew how much I loved movie house popcorn, and several times he would go into the nearby theater just to buy me popcorn as a surprise. It was very sweet of him. He would do little things like that for me. When he was nice, he was very nice.

"John loved to shop, especially at malls, and I hated to shop. I hate crowds and lines, and would rather shop in small shops. John would buy a lot of my and Bethenny's clothes. John would buy whatever she wanted, like the most expensive roller skates. He paid for horseback riding classes, but she did not care for that and gave up on the classes."

Bernadette and John stayed together until Bethenny finished high school, and the hard feelings between Bobby Frankel and John continued until Bobby was dying of cancer in 2008. John asked a mutual friend about Frankel, and sent word that he was praying for him. The friend relayed a response from Frankel: He was rooting for John, too. At the Saratoga meeting in July 2009, John inquired again and was told, "He got your message. He thanks you for your prayers and hopes you have a great meet." Bobby Frankel died in November 2009.

Bernadette, who recalled seeing her mother and father argue (fight) regularly, called her marriage to John "very volatile." Bethenny, in her 2011 *New York Times* best-seller *A PLACE of YES – 10 Rules for Getting Everything You Want Out of Life,* describes a relationship that today would be called mutually abusive. And John himself once admitted to a celebrity gossip magazine: "There were a few occasions, over the space of a year or two, when I slapped or pushed Bernadette. But I never punched Bernadette. This happened when I was taking cocaine and Bethenny was young. I regret it terribly. I also want to make it clear that I have never laid a finger on Bethenny in my entire life."

In 2017 Bernadette confirmed: " ... he did hit me. But to my knowledge John never raised his voice, let alone his hand, against Bethenny."

She said the physical abuse led to their eventual divorce. "After several police visits he was arrested and charged. In court the judge postponed judgment. John said he would give me a divorce if I dropped the charges. Despite pleas from the district attorney not to, I did. I got the divorce, too."

Owner Ted Sabarese, with whom John enjoyed his greatest successes, confirmed the chaotic home environment: "They fought all the time. I'd go over to their house and they'd be throwing things at each other. It was out of control.

"Bethenny lived through all of that."

'Bethenny Parisella'

TO SAY THAT BETHENNY FRANKEL became a big success is a lot like saying Donald Trump did "pretty well." An astute businesswoman, she created the first low-calorie category of adult beverages—Skinnygirl Cocktails—and partnered with Beam Suntory in 2011 to build the brand to include wines, flavored vodkas and ready-to-drink cocktails. By shrewdly retaining rights to the name when she sold the drink brand, she subsequently expanded Skinnygirl into a lifestyle business valued at $100 million that included products for women that offered practical solutions to everyday problems.

She also started her own TV production company, B Real Productions, which produced two seasons of the "Food Porn" show on the A&E Networks cable/satellite channel fyi, and created and produced the cable TV real estate show, "Keeping it Real Estate with Bethenny and Frederik" in which she co-starred.

Her website noted in 2018 that Bethenny also was an experienced investor; author of eight books (and counting), including five that became *New York Times* best-sellers; and a television personality whose credits included runner-up on *The Apprentice: Martha Stewart*, successful participant on ABC-TV's *Shark Tank*, cast member in Bravo's *The Real Housewives of New York City*, star of spin-off series *Bethenny Getting Married* and *Bethenny Ever After*, and host of a nationally syndicated talk show, *Bethenny*.

She was a philanthropist, too, who in late 2016 launched the "B Strong: Find Your Yes" program "designed to help women facing an unexpected hardship, such as a divorce, health issue, or eviction, with legal counseling, mental health services, and even financial assistance." She was a sought-after speaker; in 2010 she produced an exercise DVD titled *Body By Bethenny*; and in 2011 she debuted at No. 42 on Forbes Magazine's "Top 100 Most Powerful Celebrities" list.

Reading only the stories about her in national magazines and in online profiles, or watching only those episodes of her Reality TV shows dealing with her father, mother and stepfather, Bethenny's many fans understandably would believe her oft-repeated story that she overcame a miserable childhood.

"That's one of John's highs and lows," Rick Pitino said. "He treated that girl well, gave her an awful lot. But obviously they don't have a good relationship."

John often cited with distress that in an episode of her TV show *Bethenny Getting Married* she said:

"I was raised in a cave by animals."

Bethenny later wrote that she was trying to be funny with that last comment while making a point about her stormy childhood. But her attempt at humor didn't sit well with her mother or those who knew John and the privileged life he tried to provide his stepdaughter—a life that included some million-dollar houses.

"The fact that she turned out—I don't know how to put it nicely—so evil," said John's 'Bonnie,' "I don't understand it. He paid for the best schools. He made sure he went to all of her school shows. He was always there for her. And we always had a full-time housekeeper. So there was no time when she was neglected.

"If I wasn't around," Bernadette added, "it was because I was working. She was the center of our lives. For her to be so despicable is amazing to me."

There IS another side. Bethenny has said many times that John was the only father she knew, and has written that it would be dishonest to deny there were many good times, too.

Bernadette cited a few examples:

"When Bethenny was about eight years old, John and she had a comedy routine they used to do together, like Abbott and Costello. John would pose a question to Bethenny, like 'What is your mother's idea of a great day?' And Bethenny's answer was: 'A visit to the museum, a great Caesar salad, and either go back to the museum or read a book at the library.'

"I laughed with them, as well as at all the other funny things they would do together at my expense because most of it was true. They both would also make fun of my skinny legs, and John would call them 'chicken legs.'

"John loved the holidays," she continued, "especially Christmas. We had 15-foot ceilings in the house, so he would buy the tallest tree that would fit in the house. We would buy lots of Christmas gifts for Bethenny, where the whole living room was packed with gifts."

Among the good times that John recalled: with an opportunity to train horses in California, having her go with him even though she was only seven, as a way to provide a parental figure in her life ... repeatedly taking Bethenny to Coney Island, along the shore of the Atlantic Ocean, and eating Nathan's hot dogs ... for Bethenny's sixteenth birthday party, chartering a yacht docked at Freeport, Long Island, at a cost of fifty grand, and a hundred people, including Rick Pitino, showering her with congratulations ... as a high-school graduation present, taking her to Europe and staying at the Ritz-Carlton in London—and running into Hollywood Park president Peter Tunney, who in near astonishment asked, "What are you doing here?"

Coney Island is a residential neighborhood in Brooklyn known historically for its amusement parks and beach. Between 1880 and World War II it was the largest amusement area in the U.S., attracting several million visitors each year. At its peak Coney Island had three competing amusement parks: Luna Park, Dreamland and Steeplechase Park. Some of the area's most famous attractions were the Parachute Jump and the Thunderbolt and Cyclone roller coasters. And it was home, of course, to the original Nathan's, which grew into far more than a simple hot dog stand in a half-century.

> *Nathan's was recognized for a hundred years as the best hot dogs. It's a fixture. They have the best French fries, too.*
>
> *Bethenny was twelve, thirteen. I'd say, "C'mon, I'll take you on the rides at Coney Island." We'd go, just the two of us.*
>
> *We went on the Ferris wheel; I was quite comfortable with things that rock. I used to take her on the Thunderbolt; it wasn't as severe as the Cyclone. I went on that once. It was violent, scary. I wouldn't let her go on the Parachute.*

One of the more notable "good times" came when Bethenny was still in her teens. John took her to a U2 concert in Las Vegas, and they went backstage where John arranged for the group's lead singer, Bono, to meet Frank Sinatra.

> *So I was in Las Vegas at the time with Bethenny. The road manager for U2 was introduced to me. He asked about me because I was winning so much; he was an addicted gambler.*
>
> *Don Rickles was the opening act for Frank Sinatra at Caesar's. This was a benefit. Twenty-five thousand a head. Roger Moore was there. Class act.*
>
> *Bono told the road manager, "Talk to John and see if we can meet Frank." So the road manager says, "Do you have any way for U2 to get in to see Sinatra during this benefit?"*
>
> *I said, "Yeah. In fact, my uncle manages Don Rickles, who's the opening act. Yeah, I can get them in."*

He says, "Really? Let me tell you something. Bono's favorite singer is Frank Sinatra." I said, "What!?" This was so impressionable to me because here's a group: big-time, no drugs. Bono was one of the special people I spent time with in my life.

It came back to me that Steve Wynn couldn't get his daughter backstage. He could get her tickets, but he couldn't get his daughter backstage. So I was responsible for taking his daughter and Bethenny backstage to meet U2 and spend time back there. That was one of the experiences Bethenny had growing up because of my connections.

We're waiting outside the dressing room, and the head Mafia guy from Chicago, Sam Giancana, is in the dressing room. My uncle goes in; comes out. I'm feeling like a jerk. He goes in a second time. Comes out. Bono says, "Look, I'm from the streets. The hell with this."

My uncle goes in a third time. He actually went back a fourth time, and Sinatra came out. Shook hands and they talked.

Sinatra was a strange bird. As much as people would see in him, he wasn't really friendly. When he introduced U2 that night, he said: "They tell me U2 is in the audience. I'll be honest with you, the only U2 I know is a boat. But they tell me they're beautiful singers."

Later, when that album came out where he sang duets with people, one of them was U2 and Bono. After that, Bono said, "Please, ANYTHING I could ever do for you—EVER do for you—just let me know."

Steve Wynn, on the other hand, disappointed John.

They treated us like kings. Steve Wynn never thanked me.

When Don Rickles died—at the age of 90—in April 2017, Bethenny took to Twitter to say she had known Rickles when she was a child, and that she had been the youngest person in the audience at some of his Las Vegas shows. The Tweet attracted many responses, several deriding her for focusing on herself instead of honoring Rickles. But one stood out as a comment on her years with John: "Wow! What a life you have led!"

In *A PLACE of YES*, Bethenny wrote positively of her Vegas experience, recalling walking around as if they were in charge, feeling proud to be with John, enjoying the high-roller lifestyle. She also wrote fondly of being with John on the backside at tracks early in the morning ... of starting the day with donuts or chocolate cake. ("I'd set her up in my office in the morning," John said, "because it's too risky to be out while the horses are working out.")

Summers at Saratoga, she wrote, were the "very favorite" thing about her childhood ... the proverbial "good old days." Ted Sabarese recalled his daughter spending summers with John and Bethenny in Saratoga Springs, and recalled: "The girls were friendly and it was wonderful." John recalled: "I remember how hospitable she was to Sabarese and me in Saratoga. She made breakfast for us."

* * *

A GOOD EXAMPLE OF JOHN'S COMMITMENT to his stepdaughter is the lengths to which he went to make sure Bethenny was able to attend good schools, as Bernadette noted: "When Bethenny had to select a school after sixth grade, all of her friends were choosing the local Catholic school. She had no religious instruction previously, but she wanted to go with them."

> *I went to this school—it was a Catholic school (on Long Island)—and they told me there was a very long waiting list.*

After I spent an hour trying to get her in, they said it would be a couple years. So I met with the bishop's counterpart, Monsignor Melton. (Msgr. Edward Melton was also one of the foremost judges of jumping horses in the nation.)

I explained to him my problem.

He calls me the next day and says, "Go in tomorrow." I said, "What's going on?"

He said, "Go in tomorrow."

This is, like, three days later. Monday: "Oh, Mr. Parisella. Come in. I have these papers." So she went to school there for a while.

"She entered school," Bernadette continued, "did well, and when it came time for the class to receive Confirmation (one of the Catholic Church's sacraments), John had to call his friend, Msgr. Melton, so that she might receive Baptism and Communion first. No one at the school knew she had not been baptized or received Communion. Msgr. Melton arranged for her to be baptized and receive Communion privately at St. Agnes Cathedral in Rockville Center."

Bernadette said she had converted to Judaism before Bethenny was conceived and by the time of the event at St. Agnes was an atheist, so "I was apathetic." But, she acknowledged, "John was thrilled."

Yes, John moved around, and thus Bethenny, too. But whether it was Queens or Long Island—New York, California or Florida—John placed a priority on her education. Usually, she benefitted from his name-recognition, his persuasiveness, and, when he had it, his money.

I put her in a private school, an exclusive school. Very expensive. From Montessori, to the parochial school, to this school. You had to have money to get in.

In grammar school, for a while she changed her name to Parisella.

In *A PLACE of YES* Bethenny explained that when she was asked her name during registration at one school, it seemed inappropriate to her to say 'Frankel.' She went by Bethenny Parisella for years afterward, even though John never actually adopted her. She changed back to Frankel, she wrote, when John and Bernadette divorced.

When it was time for Bethenny to go to high school, said Bernadette, "she requested to attend Old Westbury High. Her exact words to me were, 'I want to go to football games and have a normal high school life.' John was against it, but I did not mind."

Bethenny started high school at Old Westbury, but it was apparent during her first year there that she needed a more structured environment. In one of her books, for example, Bethenny acknowledged demolishing John's Porsche before she was old enough to have a driver's license.

Bethenny was a problem growing up. It happens with teenagers.

I told Bonnie we should try to find a high school Bethenny would board at. The best boarding high school in the United States was Pine Crest (in Fort Lauderdale, Florida).

"Before she went off to boarding school," Bernadette recalled, "she asked for a car. But I didn't think she was responsible enough after what she had done with the Porsche. John insisted that she needed one down in Florida for school and bought it for her. John would give her anything she wanted. Again, I acquiesced."

In *A PLACE of YES* Bethenny also wrote of living with the sudden, seismic shifts from John The High Roller to John The Pauper, and how the uncertainty affected her. A story from John illustrates what she faced.

> *Bethenny was ready to start college. She said, "John, your credit card didn't work."*
>
> *I explained to her, "Honey, I'm broke. I'm in a lot of trouble. So there's no reason why you shouldn't try again with your father. Because I can't do anything, and I don't know how long it's going to take me to get outta this. You don't have to eat peanut butter and jelly seven days a week; you've got a rich father."*
>
> *When she started college, I worked a deal with Frankel where we transferred horses and the commissions went toward paying her tuition.*

* * *

THE BEST DESCRIPTION OF BETHENNY is her own, gleaned from two of her books:

She's not a go-along-to-get-along person who avoids conflict. She's successful, pragmatic, decisive and instinctive. Her sense of humor straddles the line between appropriate and inappropriate, sometimes cynical. She's sharp-tongued—honest to the point of bluntness.

This hard-nosed approach made it almost impossible for Bernadette or John and Bethenny to remain close.

"I haven't spoken to her in twenty years," said her mother in 2018. "The only time was when she called me and said, 'I wanted to give you a heads-up. There's going to be an article in People (magazine) that's derogatory to you.' And that was the end of the conversation. That was the only time in twenty years I've heard from her.

"I actually tried to figure out why, what could be the reason, to be so horrible. And I finally came up with a reason that I think makes sense.

The only reason I could come up with is her TV show. Her ratings were going way down. As soon as this story came out, they skyrocketed. All of a sudden she became a hit again.

"She always spent money on PR, so I'm assuming she was advised to do this by her PR people—for ratings, because it worked! Her books started selling; her ratings went up; she became famous. I don't know if I'm right or wrong, but it's the only thing I could come up with that made any sense at all."

John's disappointment is evident in his comments about the empty years that followed.

> *When Bethenny went off to college, I never heard back from her. I always wanted to maintain a relationship with her—here's a girl I raised from the time she was two years old. She went her own way and did whatever she had to do to be successful.*
>
> *I treated her like gold, but she built her reputation on growing up in caves instead of million-dollar houses and private schools. She had to run away from me.*
>
> *Then I get that phone call (in 2010). "I feel awkward, and I'm sure you do too, but I want to get together with you." It felt so good that she tried to reach out to me.*
>
> *She wanted me to meet her husband and everything. I said, "That's great. I look forward to that. I'm so happy you called."*
>
> *I went out to dinner twice, with her and her husband, and then the relationship wasn't pursued by her. Inside of me I saw the same Bethenny I saw twenty years before—even more so because she was a success. The conversation didn't lead to any kind of appreciation whatsoever.*

> *When the baby (daughter Bryn) was born, I congratulated Bethenny. I bought a present for Bryn's two-year-old birthday party. We went to the park prior to that. But she couldn't tell her daughter anything about me. In truth, there's nobody who exists in Bethenny's life who could tell her daughter anything about her growing up.*

Despite it all, John never stopped showing his concern for his stepdaughter. When Bethenny nearly died from a food allergy in mid-December 2018 ("I couldn't talk, see, thought I had a stroke and was dying," she was quoted in a story in an online report.), John reached out.

> *I remembered when Bethenny was a teenager, her having a bad reaction to fish she had eaten. I was so worried then because she broke out all over her body. So when I heard about the report in the news, I was worried.*

> *I texted her, "I'm so happy you're feeling better and made it through. Thank God." She didn't respond; I knew she wouldn't. But I'm not going to stop being me. .*

Perhaps something Bethenny wrote in *A PLACE of YES* helps to explain this confusing, conflicted part of John's life.

While pointing out the erratic environment of her youth, she acknowledged that John was there for her and loved her like his own child. She said she loved John, and also said she wanted him to know that, for a long time, she thought of him as her dad (even though she did not try to have any type of father-daughter relationship as an adult).

Ups and Downs

IN HIS ALL SAINTS DAY HOMILY one year, a parish priest told his congregation: "The definition of a saint is someone with a past." His point was that even those who make the Heavenly Hall of Fame were human, and thus, far from perfect. If he's got it right, that message of hope means John Parisella—using his favorite way of expressing such things—has a shot.

John definitely messed up in his otherwise successful life in many different ways, particularly after he became Bethenny Frankel's stepfather. Besides a serious gambler (he estimates he was broke "close to a dozen times"), he did drugs for roughly a decade, sometimes drank too much, knowingly bounced checks, and married and divorced more than once.

"I've never seen a person with the emotional ups and downs he's gone through," said his friend Jimmy Alexander (nicknamed Clipboard by John because he always carried a clipboard when he was at the track), "the physical ups and downs ... the financial ups and downs. They are things you'd think would cause you to be hospitalized for mental exhaustion. But he was at the barn, every day, in with his horses.

"Other trainers would ask me, 'How does he do it?' The term unique is very over-used. People misuse it all the time, say 'This is unique.' No. Unique means only one. That is the origin of unique. John is unique."

Yet throughout his tumultuous career, John was a generous friend and willing intermediary, always going to bat for his friends.

John Nash, who was general manager of four pro basketball

teams (Philadelphia, Washington, New Jersey and Portland) as well as a Thoroughbred owner, illustrated this point with an anecdote from his NBA career.

"I remember when I was with the Nets. I was approached by the Sixers to come back, and the Nets did not want to allow me out of my contract. John called Joe Taub, one of the owners, who he knew from being his trainer, and he was giving Joe what-for on the phone. I had no interest in having him do that because I was under contract and Joe had treated me very well. Subsequently, they didn't allow me to leave, but they tore up my contract and gave me a new deal, and I think, in part, John was probably responsible for that.

"I wouldn't have used his style, but it was very effective. And that was John. He would take up the cause for anybody he thought was being mishandled. He would argue with authority. He was never one to cringe in the presence of authority. He's one of the greatest people I've ever encountered. One of the all-time characters, but he's got the biggest heart in the world."

No one helped John through his financial ups and downs more than Ken Dunn, who repeatedly covered for him when he wrote checks that had no funds behind them, once guaranteed John's purchase of some much-needed racing stock, and years later helped him buy houses. "I would have been out of the game if I hadn't had Ken Dunn in my life," John said, citing examples:

> *I sat down with him and said, "I'm dead broke. You're one of my best friends, and I'm asking a favor. I have to kite checks.*
>
> *If I have to bounce a check, I have to bounce it with you." I kited checks seven, eight times.*
>
> *I bought three horses for about $52,000. I had no money. I made this deal with Ken, to run the horses—don't forget: I always had the reputation of always being a winner—and all*

the money from purses would all go to the Ocala Breeders Sale. Ken guaranteed that I would pay.

The horses won, and I paid back the fifty thousand.

* * *

THE "DOWNS" BEGAN SHORTLY AFTER John's appearances on "The Tonight Show With Johnny Carson." "Several of my close friends were doing drugs," he said of the cadre of Hollywood names who became his pals at the height of his "Trainer To The Stars" days.

The record confirms the challenge John faced. From those eighty-six winners (in 442 starts, or 19.4%) and earnings of more than a half-million dollars in 1973 (equal to more than three million in 2018), he stumbled to only sixty-two starts, seven winners (11.3%) and earnings of less than seventy-five thousand dollars in 1978. His combined win totals for the four years between 1976 and 1979 didn't equal 1973.

"I don't have a clue about years," he answered when asked to place certain events in a timeline from the mid-Seventies to the early Eighties. And forget names. What he could recall, though, graphically documents the depths of his demise during that period.

> I'm absolutely broke with no place to live in Hollywood—no place to go. I always had black friends, and this time one of them introduced me to one of the biggest drug dealers in Hollywood. Hollywood Park is one of the worst neighborhoods you could ever live in.
>
> I still had a high profile—my name meant something—but I was down. He said, "What are you doing?" I said, "Just hanging around." He said, "C'mon, let's go to dinner."
>
> After dinner, he said, "Let me drop you off; where you living?"

I said, "I'll be honest with you. I have no place to go. I have to figure something out."

He said, "You're coming home with me."

I lived with him for seven months. I can't remember his name, but he became one of my best friends ever.

He took me to parties with him. I remember there were some blacks there from Tennessee, and I know they had guns on them. And in their hearts they wanted to pull the guns out and shoot me. They were bad dudes. But my friend didn't care. Out of respect for him, because he was so big in the drug industry, they weren't going to cross him. He was making them money.

This other time there were two other drug dealers, and they were knocking me and everything. So he turned to them, and said, "You guys are so tough. How about a challenge with my whitey friend. You guys like cocaine; he does cocaine. You put up ten thousand apiece, and I'll put up twenty thousand. Let's see who's the last one standing."

We sat in this apartment, very seclusive, at a table, and we started doing the drugs. One guy lasted almost the entire day, then he cracked up. The second guy lasted almost two days. Then he crapped out. I'm still going, talking on the phone, and my friend's laughing because those two guys were out of it.

This is the kind of guy he was: He gave me half the winnings. It wasn't the money. I was his friend and he loved me; he couldn't wait to show these guys up.

One day he gave me five thousand and a ticket, and said "Get on this plane tomorrow because I'm going to get raided." He

> *didn't want me to get caught up in his troubles. The following day they raid him and put him in jail. I never saw him again.*
>
> *I went to San Francisco and was found, passed out on the streets, by a stranger who took me in. Then a girl helped me out. I was broke and she had money. I was totally out of it. I was doing cocaine and Quaaludes. Tried mescaline, but I didn't do a couple other heavy things. Never a needle.*

* * *

BILL SHOEMAKER IS ACKNOWLEDGED TO HAVE been one of the greatest jockeys in racing history. He WON eight thousand, eight hundred, thirty-three races, including the Kentucky Derby four times, the Preakness twice and the Belmont Stakes five times—eleven Triple Crown victories in all. He rode John's horses more than twenty times, but never more memorably than one day at Del Mar, the seaside track located twenty miles north of San Diego, when John was in one of his down-and-almost-out periods.

> *I was running a horse at Del Mar, and you couldn't be more broke than I was. This horse in no way could lose, so I went to Harry Silbert (Bill Shoemaker's agent throughout his career) and I said, "Harry, I hope you have nothing in this race because my horse can't lose." He said, "Sure, John, it's no problem." Harry Silbert was renowned as one of the greatest agents in the game.*
>
> *In the paddock, I said, "Mr. Shoemaker, I really appreciate you accepting this mount, but I have to share this with you: I don't have a dollar left in my pocket. I bet three hundred on this horse, so all I'm just letting you know is I don't believe that this horse can lose."*
>
> *He said, "Okay, fine, that's good."*

So he got on the horse, and it might have been one of the worst rides of his career. The horse should have won by four or five lengths, and it got beat a couple lengths. So now he comes back—and I had no relationship with him—and he's getting off the horse and he says, "I'm sorry."

I said, "You're sorry? You're Shoemaker, riding a horse for me, and I had that privilege. No. Thank you, for the honor of accepting my mount."

I'm walking out and his valet runs up to me and says, "Bill said to stop by the jockey's room." I had no idea why. He comes running down the stairs and he hands me an envelope. And in it is five hundred-dollar bills!

Another time Shoemaker made John's day by NOT riding as intended.

We're at Santa Anita. He had ridden my best horse and won two in a row on him. He was a decent horse, and he ran for good purses.

He calls Harry Silbert late the night before the race, or early in the morning, and says, "That horse is a tough horse to ride, and out drinking all night, I can't do him justice. But tell John not to worry about it. Tell him to put whomever he wants on that horse, as long as he picks a jockey who will let him run."

So after the race, Harry calls Shoemaker to tell him the horse won. Shoemaker says, "I already know he won because I was standing on the backside, rooting for the kid."

Shoemaker's last victory came on January 20, 1990, at Gulfstream. Two weeks later he rode his last race, a fourth-place finish at Santa Anita.

Later that year he was chosen the first living recipient of the New York Racing Association's Mike Venezia Memorial Award, which had been established the year before and presented posthumously to jockey Mike Venezia, its namesake, who was killed in a racing accident at Belmont Park in October 1988. The award is presented to a jockey for "extraordinary sportsmanship and citizenship."

* * *

AFTER JOHN MARRIED BERNADETTE BIRK and became Bethenny Frankel's stepfather, he bought a luxury home in Old Westbury, Long Island, not too far from the site of the barn fire a few years earlier. Nothing better illustrates the ups-and-downs of John's life than this episode.

> *I bought the house for three hundred seventy-five thousand. This was the house that Bonnie and I lived in, and Bethenny was growing up in.*
>
> *The broker wouldn't bring my bid in; I brought my own bid in because she told me it was too low. "It's embarrassing," she said. The old people liked me and accepted it. She was just looking for money.*
>
> *There were, like, eleven things wrong with the house. Bonnie's an interior and architectural designer. We were able to paste a lot of things together to cover up for the engineering. She did a great job.*

By the late 1980s John had to sell. The eventual buyer was New York radio "shock jock" Howard Stern.

> *Howard Stern's supposed to be a big name. I don't like him; don't like what he stands for. But as soon as he walked in, his opening remark was, "My father is a big fan of yours, and*

loves horse racing." He's nice to me even though I can't stand him. I like that in my life, to be recognized.

I just back off. My life's on the line. If I don't sell this house, I have to go hide. I have to sell this house.

We go to the closing. Howard Stern is brash; he's arrogant; he's obnoxious. Unfortunately, I have a temper. Because of his actions, I walk out. I'm the dumbest man in the world, an idiot.

My lawyer comes running out after me, because he wasn't getting paid unless we sold the house. He brings me back to the table, and we make certain concessions. Sold the house for a million-three.

On the radio for months after that, Stern is complaining, "I bought this house and everything's falling down." No names were mentioned, but he carried on for three months. And it was the truth, because we pasted it together.

Years later Bethenny called Stern's radio show. He seemed unaware of her connection to John until she brought up the house, mentioning that Stern had kept John's name on the mailbox for some time after the sale. At that Stern said he recalled meeting her as a girl and remembered that John was a Thoroughbred trainer, but he didn't revive his complaints about the house.

* * *

AS JOHN'S CAREER TEETERED ON the edge of oblivion in the late 1970s, he met Morris Bailey, who was part of a group that hired John to be its horse trainer. What ensued was a life-changing, lifelong friendship.

"I met him because of horse racing," Bailey said. "I had never been to a track, into my thirties. I got a group of young guys to put in a couple thousand apiece to go claim a horse. That introduced me to the racetrack, and I was hooked.

"We chipped in and got other horses, and ended up with John as our trainer. He was our second trainer. He was young, dynamic—flamboyant, for sure—and had an excitement about him. Most importantly, he was very smart and a great trainer.

"I've had real exciting times with him. He's a real talent, one of the top training personalities in the business."

> *We met each other through a friend of his. His friend wasn't with me but wanted to go into the horse game. He asked Morris to be his partner. The friendship developed.*
>
> *They went partners on a $7,500 horse, and wound up having three cheap horses. I was unbelievably successful for them. One horse that I only paid ten thousand for won nine out of ten.*
>
> *Joe Taub—owner of the Nets—his veterinarian said to get rid of the horse, and I knew the horse. Nice To Have was her name. Joe thought he was making a score, and he wanted to kill himself when she started winning. I knew the horse had a problem with the knee and I could take care of it.*

Born in Atlantic City, Bailey, his six siblings and mother moved to Brooklyn when he was fourteen, after his father died. He started into business at the age of 20, operating go-carts at Coney Island. He and two buddies who were his partners then built a concession stand, which led to three fast-food restaurants in New York and New Jersey, which Bailey eventually turned into fifty-two Burger King restaurants.

Bailey sold the franchises in the early 1990s to concentrate on his New York City real estate empire, which got its start in 1983 when he bought the Westinghouse Building near City Hall—with a loan from John, who by then had signed a lucrative contract to train for Ted Sabarese.

Bailey "was embarking on a career with investment in real estate," John said, "and his brother backed out so it left him in a hole. I was able to help." Bailey's JEMB Realty Corp. would grow to own more than $4 billion in assets (hotels, resort properties, commercial office space and residential buildings), mostly in New York, Philadelphia and Montreal.

More than anyone else at the time, Morris Bailey saved John from himself.

"John had his issues," Bailey said. "Very high-strung ... got involved in situations he shouldn't have gotten involved in. But I bonded with him. I looked at him like family after a while. He was exciting and I liked him. He's a very formidable guy, a real talent."

It would be hard to find two people with more contrasting lifestyles. Privacy and relative anonymity were priorities for Bailey throughout his life. A family man, he was proud to say in 2018 that he had been married to same woman for 56 years, and even prouder that his family included nine grandchildren.

"Early on I really tried to work with him and get to reality," said Bailey, who at one point told John he couldn't allow John to be responsible for his horses after John said he honestly couldn't say he had stopped using drugs. "He was problematic, right, with drugs, gambling and all the vices that destroy a person. I felt very badly for him, and I reached out to him. There's no question I was a positive influence in his life.

"I made it clear to him that if that's what he was going to be, a track bum who's going to take every penny and bet on the horses, he had to look around and see what he was going to be. Either that or make a decision in life and stop it. I just let him know that he was destroying his life. He was too smart to accept that."

Years later, John would do for a young trainer named Anthony Margotta Jr. what Morris Bailey did for him.

Backstretch

Previous page: Churchill Downs' famous twin spires and John Parisella talking with Angel Cordero on the backside *(photo courtesy of John Parisella)*

Claim to Fame

IN AN OFF-THE-CUFF HORSE RACING primer called *Stuff About Steeds*—published the year John Parisella was born—the author, a New York handicapper, began Chapter Two by explaining the claiming race, which he termed "a necessary evil" in what John came to call The Racing Game. The vast majority of Thoroughbreds, the author wrote, were considered "platers" because of the poor condition of their legs. Each plater was assigned a selling price and ran in a claiming race, and could be "claimed" for that price by anyone who had started a horse at a track.

Had the writer been John's contemporary, he easily could have been referring specifically to the man who, decades later, became one of the New York Racing Association's best-known trainers—both for his success with claimers, as platers became known, and his undisputed prowess as a "foot man."

"Parisella's horses, for the most part, have $12,500-down-to-$10,000 written all over them," retired *Sports Illustrated* senior editor William Leggett, a respected Thoroughbred racing authority, wrote in 1995 for *Thoroughbred Times*. He was referring to the stock in John's barn at Aqueduct that spring, but his words acknowledged the virtual miracles John performed with claimers most of his career. That success was the stuff of legend, almost always related to John's gift for working with a horse's feet.

Ken Dunn, who became a very good friend of John's as their careers progressed, recalls a classic example from when Dunn was in his first general manager position, at Atlantic City. That New Jersey track, which closed in 2015, was owned at the time by Bob Levy, a 2005 inductee into the Philadelphia Sports Hall of Fame, and his dad, Dr. Leon Levy, who with William S. Paley co-founded the CBS television network. The Levys operated what Dunn termed "a very nice racing stable" (Robert P. Levy Stables) whose horses earned several Eclipse Awards and one, Bet Twice, won the Belmont in 1987. Their trainer was eventual Hall of Famer Warren A. (Jimmy) Croll.

"John shows up at Atlantic City," Dunn recalled, "and he's got four claiming horses. He's living in a little place on the Black Horse Pike called Rose's Cabins, staying with an exercise girl because she's got a car and he doesn't. She's taking him back and forth to the racetrack.

"With these four claiming horses," Dunn said, "John wins about 16 races."

But that's not the best part of this story.

"I believe he won the only match race in the history of Atlantic City Race Track," Dunn said. "I had carded a six-horse field, and it scratched down to two. We were mandated to run it. I refused to run it in front of the public, but I still had to pay the purse money. We had this little program on Saturday morning. John stays in the race; it's a $14,000 claimer. He stays in the race and wins by a sixteenth of a mile.

"John needs money," Dunn continued, "and he's got this $14,000 claiming horse. He cuts up with Bob Levy all the time, just playing with him, teasing him and ribbing him. He needs some money, so he sells Bob this $14,000 claiming horse.

"Bob gives him to Jimmy Croll to train, and two weeks later Bob comes to me and says, 'Ken, what'd your friend do to me? Jimmy Croll said this horse has such bad feet, he's crippled. He'll never run.'

"I called John and said, 'Do you know what kind of a spot you put me in after I recommended that he buy this horse from you? His trainer says he'll never run.'

"John says, 'I'll tell you what. Tell Bob I want the horse, and he can have what it wins. John took the horse and went to New York and won—several straight."

I couldn't give the money back. I sold the horse because it was one of the worst times, financially, for me.

So I said to Ken, "I don't have the money; you know that's why I sold the horse. Let them give me the horse, and I'll take it to New York and I won't charge them anything, and I'll win with this horse."

I went to Bob and said what I proposed. He's got a Hall of Fame trainer telling him the horse is lame, but what could he do? So he sent the horse to New York.

I won three straight at Belmont then gave it back to them. I told Ken the problem was with his feet. I just took care of them.

"John was a big believer in taking special care of the horse's feet," Dunn recalled. "He recognized that you have to build from the bottom up. There were times he would train horses without shoes completely until they were able to grow the foot out. He was a great believer in feet and legs. That's why he was so successful, particularly, with claiming horses, with horses that others wanted to cast off and didn't think had a value because they weren't running well. John would take those horses and, many, many times, start with the feet and their legs, and the next thing you knew, he had taken horses that were basically throwaways and was winning races."

Perhaps the best example of John's prowess with horses' feet involves Country Day, a top three-year-old in 1990. A candidate for The Kentucky Derby, Country Day came up lame after an impressive workout at Churchill Downs. The fear was that the colt had suffered a hairline fracture in a leg, or at least a sprain. John determined that the horse was reacting to a hard track, and fitted him with rubber shoes. A few weeks later—in what was considered a miracle in racing circles—Country Day ran second in the Peter Pan Stakes at Belmont Park, then went to the post in the Belmont Stakes, the third leg of the Triple Crown, on June 9.

* * *

JIMMY CLIPBOARD WAS ACTIVE IN RACING himself from the time he started handicapping when he was nine years old. Jimmy was well-known around the track for being, in John's words, "a successful gambler on the New York circuit for forty years," and many people went to him for advice and tips on races. While working at the New York City headquarters of ABC TV as a 19-year-old, he was Howard Cosell's source of expert information whenever Cosell covered a horse race for the network. "He didn't want anybody saying, 'You don't know what you're talking about,'" Alexander said. Jimmy obtained his groom's license in 1983 and his assistant trainer's license three years later. After John retired, Clipboard fervently argued that John Parisella belonged in the National Museum of Racing and Hall of Fame at Saratoga.

"He profoundly changed the way horses were trained, maintained and cared for through injuries," Jimmy Clipboard said. "John was the first trainer to cut out the frog of the horse's hoof to remove foreign substances and allow the frog to grow back stronger. He used glue-on shoes for horses that had hoof problems and brittle hooves—something he learned from Campo." Added Ted Sabarese, for whom John trained exclusively through most of the 1980s and saddled his best-known horses: "We were using the magnets on the horse's hind quarters before that was thing to do."

Those long hours in stalls before John became a trainer—lessons he learned from Tommy Gullo and John Campo—turned into his trademark. "In the morning," said Jimmy Clipboard, "he'd go in the stall, get down on his knees—every horse—and look at them, feel their legs, because things could change in a day, change in a minute. He'd run his hands down the horse's legs to detect subtle changes or differences. He'd rub their legs and watch their ears. A horse's ears are very important. They use them to balance their weight. Their ears will move the same way they move their weight. When he went to the back of a horse, he would watch the horse's tail.

"John was so in tune with the horse," Clipboard continued. "Other trainers, if they have a problem with a horse, the first thing they do is call the vet. John would feel their legs and wait. Top trainers couldn't run their hands down a horse's legs and know. He could diagnose problems no other trainer could pick out. He did it in a way no other trainers did, because he did everything by eye. No matter whether it was a cheap horse, good horse, stakes horse—he knew the horse top to bottom."

Sabarese saw that keen horse sense up close. "John could spot a problem coming. He'd tell me, 'I see this horse is off a little on the left front. We're going to have a problem on the right rear.' And a week later, we would. I had a great trainer, who worked his tail off and definitely improved the horses, definitely."

> *I learned so much about the feet from Campo. In vet school they just spend a matter of hours on a horse's feet. John was known for doing work on the feet. He was a genius. He learned from his boss, Eddie Neloy, when it comes to a horse's feet.*
>
> *John was the number-one trainer in the game, and that was his number-one go-to asset. He said it was the most important thing. So that's what I did. I worked on the horse's feet, because that affected ankles, shoulders—so much about the horse.*
>
> *There would be bruises underneath there in the frog, and they were neglected by most. In cutting them out, they'd bleed a little bit. And no trainer wanted to see that. It scared them to death. But it was good for the horse.*

> *I learned that from Campo and took that to Turfway Park with me. To be more creative, I trained without shoes there. I might have been the only trainer in Kentucky that trained without shoes. When they reached the point where the ankles weren't sore, I put shoes on them and jogged them.*

John's practice of training horses without shoes was met with incredulity from most trainers. There's no better example of disbelief than that exhibited in 1996 by Dale Romans, who won the 2011 Preakness with Shackelford and upset Triple Crown winner American Pharoah at Saratoga with Keen Ice in 2015.

> *While in Kentucky I trained my horses without shoes because I did a lot of work on their frogs so I just wanted to send them out in bandages to cover them up.*
>
> *Dale Romans, a prominent trainer, as well as his father for decades, turned to me and said to me—and we were friendly: "John, they tell me you're training without shoes. I can't believe that. Nobody trains without shoes and wins. So I can't believe that."*
>
> *I said, "What do you want me to do?"*
>
> *He said, "Make me a believer. Let me come in your barn and let me pick up a horse's legs. But," he says, "I want to pick out my horse. I'll make the pick." In other words, he didn't want me showing him one horse without shoes.*
>
> *He walked into the barn and, however many horses there were, he walked up the line and he picked out this one horse. No shoes. Another, no shoes. Another, no shoes.*
>
> *He left just shaking his head. No remark. He still didn't believe it even after he saw it.*

Fueled by his unmatched ability to treat horses' feet, John's record as a trainer includes some almost unimaginable achievements. Overall, his horses finished in the money 44.8% of the time in 6,770 starts (949 seconds and 840 thirds to go with his 1,241 firsts). He WON at least ONE RACE ... EVERY YEAR for FORTY-EIGHT YEARS—1969 through 2016.

On March 8, 1972 he saddled three winners at Aqueduct, one in Pennsylvania and one in New Jersey—five on the same day, in three states. (The three at Aqueduct were horses he had claimed in their previous races.)

"He's a brilliant horseman," said John Nash. "He had a knack for identifying and evaluating horses. His regimen was somewhat different, but very effective. John trained at the highest levels, as well as at my level, which is the not-so-expensive horses."

John was the leading trainer at the 1980 Aqueduct Winter-Spring meeting with twenty-one firsts in fifty-two starts, a .404 winning percentage. Three years later, he won thirteen of twenty-one starts (a .619 winning percentage), and in 1985 at Belmont Park, also in the winter, he had fifteen winners in twenty-six starts (a .577 winning percentage). He went to Turfway Park in Florence, Kentucky in 1996 with six horses and $50,000 for claims, and set a track record for wins by one trainer in a meet with forty.

By then, Rick Pitino had become a close friend. And, believe it or not, John learned something from the coach that made him a more successful judge of prospective claimers.

> *What made me better was all the time I spent with Rick Pitino, because they were constantly watching film. So my first key was to keep watching the video replays of the horse's previous race. I was doing it before, but being around Rick made me much more intense about the significance of that.*
>
> *The first thing anybody looks for is if the horse changes leads, because if he stays on one lead, he usually has a problem. If*

he can't put pressure on one leg, it means something is hurting him—unless he's in the hands of a very low-percentage trainer.

John learned something else by watching Pitino run his team's practice: how to be more effective and productive around his barn. "I'm easily distracted," he told a reporter. "His focus, which stems from intensity, leaves me in awe. Sometimes I daydream. I don't think this guy allows himself to daydream. By being able to be focused, he can get a lot done. I try to prepare for my daily routine like Rick."

Running for the Roses

IT IS NEARLY EVERY HORSEMAN'S DREAM to be standing in the Winner's Circle at Churchill Downs as the blanket of red roses is draped over the latest winner of the Kentucky Derby. And John Parisella was no exception. He called it "the one race I couldn't wait for as a kid growing up. It was all you knew: The Kentucky Derby. Period."

The iconic horse race has been run every May since 1875, with more than 150,000 people attending the race each year in recent times. Traditions abound: the mint julep, burgoo, Derby pie, lavish Easter Bonnet-like ladies' hats, the "Rider's Up" call, the playing of "My Old Kentucky Home" and, of course, the blanket of roses—a tradition dating to the 1800s. The Derby even inspired a song, "Run for the Roses" by Dan Fogelberg—with the unforgettable line "the chance of a lifetime, in a lifetime of chance"—released in 1980. The Derby winner that year was the first filly since Regret in 1915—Genuine Risk, trained by one of John's close friends, Leroy Jolley Sr.

The next best thing to winning the "Run For The Roses" is to send your Thoroughbred onto the track to the strains of "The sun shines bright on my old Kentucky home ..." as John did with Fight Over in 1984. To have your horse contending at the head of the stretch run—as Fight Over did—is a bonus thrill.

Running in The Derby was just one of many highlights during the years John trained for Ted Sabarese, who said, "I was not in the horse racing business. I had a computer company and it grew to be a pretty big company." They became a team in 1983, but not before John cleared a couple of hurdles: Ted's cousin, who wanted to be a trainer, and Ted's initial resistance to John's loyalty to an old friend.

> *His cousin on his father's side went to three trainers. This guy wanted to be very much involved. All three trainers said, "We don't want any part of it."*
>
> *The third trainer was a close friend of mine, and we loved playing jokes on each other. He said, "The guy you should go to is Parisella"—playing a joke!*
>
> *I know this guy and what he's made of, but what am I going to do? I'm broke. He thought I'd throw the guy out.*
>
> *With that, Sabarese has to meet me before he puts up any money. We go to Jersey; this guy takes me all around Jersey and gets lost. I said, "I can't do this. Let me go home."*
>
> *We wound up at Sabarese's office, and he cuts me a check for $25,000.*
>
> *I said, "Listen to me, Ted. You're giving me twenty-five thousand. It's like throwing it in the street. I'm not in the game."*
>
> *He said, "How much would you like?"*
>
> *I said, "I need seventy-five thousand."*
>
> *He went back and wrote me a check for $75,000.*
>
> *I got on a big roll for Sabarese right away. Once I got on that roll, the cousin came in and said, "I'm going to do this and I'm going to do that."*
>
> *I said, "I want you out of my barn."*

He says, "Well, I'm going to get you fired."

I said, "I can't do this. I'm not going to let you run the barn, be the boss."

Sabarese called me. He said, "John, what's the problem?"

I said, "Ted, listen to me. You're a great owner and it's a shame, but I have to do this, because he wants to run over me and be boss in the barn."

Ted said, okay, and hung up the phone. I didn't know where I stood. He called me back an hour later and said, "He's fired. I don't want him anywhere near our barn."

Sabarese's version varies only slightly, with the same outcome: "Parisella calls me up and says, 'You're cousin's a bum. I'm throwing his ass outta here.' I said, 'John, don't do that. Let me come out there.' So I went out there. One thing led to another and we went to Florida and we bought twenty-five yearlings. That was my first foot in the water with horse racing.

"Basically, the horses weren't worth a crap," Sabarese said. "We then claimed or bought a couple of running horses, and they performed. John's a very good trainer. He's got an excellent eye. He immediately moves them up with the way their feet are treated."

Ted wanted to lock up John exclusively, and proposed the most lucrative contract in racing—a million dollars a year. But John just wouldn't dump Red Byer, not even for a million dollars. Red was the older gentleman John had met one day at Belmont when someone asked him, as a favor, to spend some time with "a guy who would find it a privilege that a horse trainer would talk to him."

I had three horses for Red. Sabarese says, "I'm paying you all this money; you can't have any horses for anybody else."

I said, "Ted, this man, who you would love, doesn't interfere, has looked after me with three horses where I had nothing and wouldn't even be in the game, so I'm not going to give him up."

He says, "Then we have no deal."

A week goes by. A week! And then he says to me, "John, how do you still feel?"

So I in turn said to him. "Listen to me. Let's be fair. You're a hundred and ten percent right. It's just me, the way I'm made, who I am. But you're a hundred and ten percent right. Just do me this favor, then you to make the final decision. I want you to meet the man."

And he met Red Byer, salt of the earth; he loved him. And he loved him and he really wanted him for all the races he had. And I kept the three horses.

"I can picture Red and his wife," Sabarese said decades later. "Red was a terrific person, a wonderful kind of person. He would join us for lunch every Saturday and Sunday in the Trustees Room. He was always around, and whatever John wanted to do was fine with me."

Another time John turned down one of the biggest names in horse racing, Frank Stronach. The wealthy Austrian-Canadian owned the 1980 Canadian Horse of The Year, Glorious Song, and later owned horses that won the 1997 Belmont Stakes, 2000 Preakness and 2004 Breeders' Cup Classic. He built North America's largest Thoroughbred racing company, Stronach Group. Among the U.S. tracks owned and operated by that company were Santa Anita, Golden Gate Fields, Gulfstream and Pimlico. But John was never tempted.

He sent a helicopter to my barn and flew me up to his home in Canada. He was in the process of offering me a job, and he brought me into his library.

There were about fifty pictures in his library, and all I saw were pictures of himself. I thought, uh-oh, here we go.

I said, "Frank, you are the greatest for this game. But as far as you and I, I don't want to start something that we're not going to finish. You and I, we both have our own ideas and everything. I have so much respect for you, I don't want to go off on anything negative." He understood.

As Sabarese got better acquainted with John and realized the great things John could accomplish with horses, he set his sights higher.

"We won a few races, but nothing pizzazzy," he said. "So I said, 'John, this is no fun. You've got a good eye; I recognize that. You've moved the horses up, these claimers. Let's try to buy some good horses, some stakes horses.' He thought that was a good idea. We started going to places nobody went to. We went to Canada first, bought some stakes horses, $150,000-$200,000 per horse. (One was the eventual Don Rickles.)

"John said, 'Give me thirty to sixty days to move these horse up.' Bang! The horses started winning stakes. We went to England and did the same thing. We went to California; we got some horses there. We became very successful. We dominated the New York stakes winter racing program."

John picked his spots, Sabarese said, running every Saturday and Sunday during the winter meetings at Aqueduct and Belmont. "Every Saturday, every Sunday, we'd be having late lunch in the Trustees Room," Sabarese said, "and we'd be 1-to-5, 2-to-5, 3-to-5. We'd be the overwhelming favorite, and we generally ran well."

For five years in a row, Sabarese was the leading stakes-winning owner in New York—including twenty-four stakes victories between 1983 and 1985. He and John became regulars on Frank Wright's Saturday night horse racing show on New York City television. Recalled John: "Frank Wright said, 'You guys have been on the show so much, I may change it to the John Parisella show.'" Said Sabarese: "They were writing about me on the back page of *The Racing Form* every week. The artist there was doing cartoons of me in the racing silks. We had a lot of fun. I'd go out at five in the morning to watch John. He and I became very friendly. The success just kept rolling on."

The two represented quite a departure from the usual owner-trainer pairing common to big-time horse racing.

"We were the blue-collar guys," Sabarese said. "Picture the two of us, hanging out. I'm from New Jersey, but I'm just a regular kind of person. John talked like a Brooklyn guy; he acted like a Brooklyn guy. He took no bullcrap. If he thought I was wrong, he didn't kiss my ass. He'd say, 'You're wrong. You don't know what you're talking about.'

"I couldn't get into the big room in New York one time because I had jeans on. John had to track down one of the waiters and borrow one of the pants with the stripes down the leg. Multiply that by everywhere we went. We were unique.

"We'd go to a sale and buy a hundred yearlings. Everybody kissed our ass. We went to every farm, every luncheon and dinner. We knew everyone, or at least everyone knew us; that's for sure. John loved it because he was getting the attention he never could get in New York even though he was a great trainer and had good success and had good horses. He could never get the kind of respect one of the bluebloods would get."

Sabarese experienced first-hand John's racing idiosyncrasies and was able to manage it.

"He would make me call the Racing Secretary's office when they would give him a weight he didn't like, and bitch and moan about it. I finally said, 'That's it, John. I'm not going to call anymore.' I said, 'John, what are you, nuts? They assigned a weight. Because I yell, they're going to change the weight? Never happen.'

"John was always so particular about what post position he got. If it was a sprint and he drew the one post: 'I hate it. I'm going to scratch.' Of course, he didn't.

"He was so emotional about this stuff—every single item. If we loaded and we were in an early post position, and there were twelve to fourteen horses and we stood in the gate ... every kind of story like that. Any possible thing that could bother him would bother him. 'The track is soft on the inside, we gotta tell the jockey to stay in the middle.' I'm not saying he was wrong. He was superstitious."

Their obvious progression, said Sabarese, was: "Geez, let's win The Kentucky Derby." But, of course, that's much easier said than done, as Sabarese came to learn. "You can't buy the best horses when you go to the sales," he said, "because the big farms keep the best horses for themselves and race them."

That's not to say the two didn't flirt with Derby fame. First, there was Fight Over, in the 110th mile-and-a-quarter classic. "John really loved that horse," Sabarese said, proceeding to tell how John stole the show in Louisville as he often did wherever he went.

The story begins eleven days before the Derby, seventy-eight miles away in Lexington, at scenic Keeneland. The Bluegrass Stakes, one of the last major Derby prep races, was run at Keeneland every April, and in 1984 was won by Taylor's Special, ahead of Silent King. Fight Over ran last in a nine-horse field.

"The Kentucky Derby is a full-week event," Sabarese said, "all these dinners and luncheons with highfalutin people. We were at one of the big dinners, where each trainer gets up and talks about their horse in the race. And when it's John's turn, he gets up and says: 'Yeah, we were trying to get the price up so we held the horse in that event.' You could have heard a pin drop."

The truth is a bit different.

Fight Over was one of the choices in the Bluegrass. That morning my sinuses were killing me. Fight Over's problem was his breathing.

I called Sabarese and said, "Ted, we have to scratch Fight Over. My sinuses are killing me and he can't breathe."

He said, "What? Are you nuts? How can you scratch out of this race?"

I said, "Ted, I'm tellin' you."

He said, "John, please, run the horse."

He ran one of the worst races of his life.

Derby Day was another story. Excerpts from the race chart provide the details of Fight Over's encore, when he went off at 78-1 and beat every horse that had run with him in the Bluegrass Stakes. Breathing normally, he was in second place, five lengths behind eventual winner Swale, with a quarter-mile to go, and finished seventh:

" ... Fight Over, well-placed into the backstretch, moved through along the inside nearing the far turn, raced forwardly into the stretch, then brushed with At The Threshold while tiring ... At The Threshold rallied racing into the far turn, remained a factor into the stretch while racing between horses but wasn't good enough, and leaned in slightly, brushing with Fight Over ... A foul claim against Coax Me Chad by the rider of Fight Over, for alleged interference through the stretch, was not allowed ... "

Two weeks later, in the Preakness, Fight Over ran third, again beating Bluegrass winner Taylor's Special—ridden by Bill Shoemaker—and also ahead of Kentucky Derby winner Swale, who finished seventh in a ten-horse field. As John was saddling Fight Over, he experienced what he called one of his most emotional and inspirational moments as a trainer. It came when ABC-TV sportscaster Jack Whitaker concluded an interview with him by telling a national television audience: "John, good luck, and I assure you that all of Brooklyn is cheering for you."

* * *

FIGHT OVER WOULD BE AS CLOSE as John and Ted would come to winning the big race, though it can be argued that they came closer to the Winner's Circle later that year. The Criterium Stakes at Calder was seven furlongs, run August 4, just three months after the Derby. It's a classic case of what might have been.

"John would call me," said Sabarese, "and say, 'Ted. I saw this great horse.' I always had at least a million or two in my checking account—this guy was dangerous; I had to always be ready.

"This one time he calls and says, 'Get on your plane and come down here.' He tells me about this great horse he loves. He says, 'I see this horse. We can buy him. It's not a lot of money. He's only an allowance winner, but this horse has got potential.'

"I said, 'Okay, John, whatever you want to do. I don't remember if I went down or not. But I know he was supposed to run the next Saturday. It was another allowance race.

"We're talking about wanting a Derby horse. This horse is only an allowance winner, even though he's been impressive. We said, if he wins the allowance race on Saturday, we'll buy him. Well, he gets beat, so we don't buy him."

He never, ever, questioned me on anything.

My friend, Cam Gambolati, a good friend of mine, trained the horse. He had bought him for very cheap money, and he needed the commission, the ten percent. The price was a hundred fifty thousand.

I said, "Ted, let's buy this horse before he runs. Gambolati's

> *close to me. He runs a solid ship. Nothing's wrong with the horse. I watched the videos on this horse. I really love this horse."*
>
> *Ted says, "John, I let you do everything you want. Let him run at Calder and we'll give them a little more money. But make sure he wins."*
>
> *I'm really trying to sell him. I said, "You know, the horse could get left in the gate."*
>
> *The horse winds up running a lousy race, finishes second, and that was the end of me.*

So how does this story end? "We had a deal," said Sabarese. "The horse we should have bought, and were going to buy for $250,000, was Spend a Buck."

If the name sounds familiar, it's probably because Spend a Buck won The Kentucky Derby the next year.

In 1985, after seeing Spend a Buck win the Derby, John had another near-miss when he almost bought Alysheba for Sabarese. Almost: Dorothy Scharbauer, of Valor Farm in Pilot Point, Texas, and her daughter Pam outbid John, buying Alysheba as a yearling for $500,000. Alysheba would win the 1987 Derby and Preakness, and in 1988 finish second to Ferdinand, the 1986 Derby winner, in the Breeders' Cup Classic—in a photo finish.

> *I wanted the horse, but I felt the fair price was two-fifty. You know, you go in and you gauge what you're going to spend. Going to three-fifty, I went a hundred over what I wanted. That's the only reason. I appraised him at two-fifty.*

The Boss

BY THE TIME THE YANKEES APPEARED in the postseason again (1976), John Parisella was "Trainer to the Stars, Joe Pepitone was out of baseball, and George Steinbrenner—The Boss—owned the ball club. Steinbrenner would own the Yankees for thirty-seven years, until his death at the age of 80 on the day of the All-Star Game in 2010. He was known as the bigger-than-life, win-at-all-costs, mercurial equal of the biggest Yankee names of all time. He went through twenty-three managers, including Billy Martin five times and Dick Howser, Bob Lemon, Gene Michael and Lou Pinella twice each, and saw his team win sixteen pennants and seven World Series.

Although Steinbrenner owned and raced Thoroughbreds, John said he never considered working for The Boss. But that wasn't because of Steinbrenner's history with Yankee managers.

> *With Steinbrenner, I liked him and I was a big Yankee fan. And he knew that. And as brash and bold as he may have been, he was a winner. But he had to have all the say.*
>
> *I don't have a big ego, but in horse racing it is very difficult to give an opinion if you're not qualified, no matter how successful you are in business.*
>
> *We both readily admitted from the beginning that we had strong personalities and it would never work.*

While John was never Steinbrenner's horse trainer, The Boss had plenty of interaction with him. It was 1985 when Pepitone found himself in big trouble—"guilt by association," John called it— and John sought Steinbrenner's aide on Pepi's behalf. Again, the boys' mothers were the catalyst.

Joe had been a passenger in a car when it was stopped by police in Brooklyn for running a red light. In the car police found nine ounces of cocaine, 344 Quaaludes, a free-basing kit, a gun and more than $6,000 in cash.

> *Steinbrenner went to bat for all his ballplayers. But this one he stayed out of. My mom knew that I had an association with Steinbrenner—not that I trained horses for him, but we became friends and he had a lot of respect for me because I was a winner. If I was a loser, he wouldn't have had any respect for me. But I was a big winner.*
>
> *She said, "You know, George is not helping Joe. That's what Angie told me."*
>
> *Joe's mom was scared to death because they were threatening Joe with a jail sentence. I said, "Okay. Once I know a specific day, I'll tell you, and you and Angie can come to the track." So I waited until Steinbrenner had a horse in a stakes race.*
>
> *George had a horse in a stakes race this particular day, and the Yankees were on the road, so I knew he'd be there unless he made the trip with them. I told my mom, "You and Angie come and sit outside. Worst that can happen is, if he's not there, you spend the day at the track."*
>
> *I didn't have a horse in the stakes race at that time, but I still went into the Trustees Room to look for him. Sure enough, I found him.*

I said, "George, can I talk to you for a few minutes?" He said, "Sure."

I said, "One of the things why it was so much a privilege to meet you, George, was what you stood for. Every player that played for you, you had their back. And I loved that about you. So what I don't understand is: Joe Pepitone is a beloved Yankee, and you're ignoring his mother's calls."

He says to me, "That can't be."

I said, "You know what? I thought that would be the case. Let's just say it was miscommunication. His mother's right outside, a nervous wreck because you haven't answered any of her phone calls. So our friendship's at stake here if you don't go out and talk to her and tell her you're going to help Joe."

Now he's like, "Oh, sure, sure. I'll go see her." He went out and helped her and helped Joe.

In October 1986 Joe Pepitone was convicted of two misdemeanor counts, each carrying a maximum one-year jail sentence, but was found not guilty by a jury on four more serious charges. He was sentenced to a six-month jail term at Rikers Island, with eligibility for parole after four months. He told reporters George Steinbrenner had been "a morale booster" through the ordeal.

* * *

JOHN WAS GOOD FRIENDS WITH Hall of Fame trainer D. Wayne Lukas, and that friendship was put to the test by Steinbrenner as the Pepitone saga played out.

One of the most successful trainers of all time, Lukas was still active at the age of 83. ("You young trainers get ready because I'm not retiring," he said when accepting an award in 2014.) Through 2018 he had set a record by winning fourteen Triple Crown races and was the leading trainer in the Breeders' Cup series with victories in twenty races.

> *Wayne Lukas, to me, changed racing. At that point, all the people from Kentucky had all the good horses. Wayne broke through and was able to compete and beat them. So I held him on the highest pedestal.*
>
> *In California, I would go to his barn just to be there. We weren't even friends yet. He never, ever forgot. He would ride past me on a pony, like at Saratoga, and he'd recognize it was me and come right back. He didn't do that with many trainers.*

Lukas was Steinbrenner's trainer when The Boss sought John's opinion about an upcoming race.

> *I'm in California and I have a horse later on in a big race, and George has a horse in an earlier race. We're in that special room at Santa Anita and he says, "What do you think my chances are?" I answer, "I think you have the best horse."*
>
> *His horse went off a big favorite and got beat. So he comes back up to the room, and he calls me over. Says, "You got a few minutes?" I said, "Sure," and sat down with him.*
>
> *He says, "John, on paper—forget you—other people involved told me I had the best horse. And I got beat. So, I don't want you to pull any punches with me. I want your opinion why I got beat."*
>
> *I said, "George, I'm friends with Lukas. I don't want to make a comment on a trainer I thought could have done something different. Nah-nah."*

After talking for ten minutes, I said, "Well, in my mind, it's a filly and she should have been given an extra couple of weeks. She came back too soon."

He looked at me, and all he said was, "Okay, thanks." I said, "Please."

He told Lukas.

But Lukas, being a friend of mine, didn't care. He knew what Steinbrenner was all about.

Another time John intervened with George Steinbrenner on behalf of a "little guy" on the backside, and suffered the consequences.

Somebody came to me that I knew, a guy named Marcus, and said, "John, I'm broke, and George owes me for nine months." He said, "Here are the bills. I'll let you look at them."

I looked at them, and he was broke. If he wasn't broke, I wouldn't have gotten involved.

So I called up George and said, "George! Marcus: The guy's broke! You owe him for nine months."

He says, "OK, I'll take care of it." He sent him the money within two weeks. Never took my calls again.

World Record

TWENTY-FIVE YEARS HAD PASSED since Citation won horse racing's Triple Crown in 1948. John Parisella was seven then, already industrious with his *Brooklyn Eagle* paper route; Jackie Robinson was in his second season with the Brooklyn Dodgers.

By 1973 a lot of racing fans were wondering if another Thoroughbred would ever match Citation's sweep of The Kentucky Derby, Preakness and Belmont Stakes. Then a powerful chestnut colt nicknamed Big Red showed up at Churchill Downs.

Secretariat not only won all three Triple Crown races that year, but did so in a record time for each—winning the Belmont by thirty-one lengths. In twenty-one starts over the two years he raced, Secretariat won sixteen times and finished out of the betting money only once—fourth in his first race as a two-year-old. In that one, over five-and-a-half furlongs on July 4, 1972 at Aqueduct, he was tenth at the head of the stretch and closed fast to finish a length and a quarter short of show. He was Horse of the Year as both a two-year-old and three-year-old, and is second on *BloodHorse* magazine's Top 100 Horses of the Twentieth Century, ahead of Citation but behind Man o' War (winner of twenty out of twenty-one).

Secretariat's legendary career elevates to historic significance what Simply Majestic, trained by John Parisella, accomplished in 1988. Ted Sabarese acquired Simply Majestic as a yearling after missing out on Spend A Buck and watching that horse win the 1985 Derby. Once again, John performed his magic on a seemingly lame steed.

Simply Majestic was foaled March 10, 1984 at Keswick Stables near Charlottesville, Virginia. The 547-acre estate, purchased by the Augustus family of Cleveland in 1952, bears a mention for its four decades of successful Thoroughbred breeding from the late fifties through the late nineties. Simply Majestic was one of forty-eight stakes winners produced by Keswick during that time. He went to the post forty-four times in four years, winning eighteen times, finishing in the money eleven other times, and setting a world record previously held by Secretariat.

"This horse was so much fun to watch," said Sabarese. "He would go on the lead and go head-to-head and run just blistering fractions. He was unbelievable: seven track records; earned over a million and a half. That was my best horse."

Sabarese bought Simply Majestic in 1986 at the Fasig-Tipton New York Yearling Sale at Saratoga for $575,000. "We'd buy, like, a hundred yearlings," Sabarese said, "and we had an arrangement with a farm in Ocala (Florida). The guy there would break them and send them to John when he thought they were ready.

"Red Curtin was our guy on the farm. Red called one day and said, 'I've got this horse and he shows a lot of speed. Let me send him up there.' At first John wasn't happy with him."

> *I couldn't get the horse to work. I was sick. We bought five horses, and he was the most expensive of all five that day. Half-a-million was a lot of money in the Eighties. Finally, I had to put him in a race. I told Ted, "This horse shows me nothing."*

> *Sabarese was great. He said, "Don't worry, you'll think of something."*

> *I don't remember what I did, but I was able to turn him around. He held seven track records; he won at Santa Anita, at Longacres, at Rockingham—a bunch of different tracks.*

That's the horse that both P.G. Johnson and D. Wayne Lukas said, "This is the best job of managing a horse that I have ever seen in this business." P.G. Johnson was a big-time trainer at the time, like Lukas.

Early in 1987 John sent Simply Majestic to Lukas, who ran the horse a couple times at Santa Anita then returned him to John because, according to one report, Lukas had too many good horses. It was almost a Spend A Buck tale in reverse.

I was going through a bad divorce. I had given this horse to Lukas. He got beat twenty lengths in one race so he gave it back to me. Then we break the track record—twenty-seven days apart (and win the California Derby).

"This horse was a three-year-old, and he was blossoming late," said Sabarese. "John said, 'Let's go up to Golden Gate and run in the big race up there.' It was the California Derby, the prep for northern horses before the Kentucky Derby. I said, 'Fine.' John would always check with me, and I would never overrule him. He was the trainer.

"He calls me early in the morning the day of the race, and he says, 'Ted, I got really bad news. He's lame; the horse is lame. I gotta scratch.' I said, 'Okay, whatever you gotta do, you gotta do.'

"Half an hour later he calls me back and says, 'Ted, I tried something and he's walking around pretty good. I think I'm gonna run him.' I said, 'Okay, whatever you think makes sense.'"

I think I know more about feet than most trainers. I said, "Let me try this last thing."

I pulled the heel nails out, because that was one of my tricks that I forgot to do. And all of a sudden he walked great.

Sabarese had remained in New Jersey rather than flying to California. "These were the early days of cable," he said, "and I had a big dish in my office. I was able to pick up the races. We had a bug boy on the horse so we got a break with the weight.

"The race starts and the horse lays back. They come into the turn and, like he's shot out of a cannon, he circles the field and breaks the track record and wins by about ten lengths.

"I said, 'Holy Smokes!'"

It was after Lukas returned Simply Majestic that John, as Sabarese had put it, "thought of something."

I did a lot of things from the time when Lukas got beat by twenty lengths. To me the horse's knee was bothering him. The veterinarian said there's nothing wrong with his knee. I said, "Okay, good, inject the knee anyway."

What they do, when they inject the joints, is draw fluid out and shoot cortisone back in.

The vet thought I was nuts. I experienced that many times in my career: The veterinarian thought I was wrong. There's an old adage I was taught: If you're going to let the veterinarian call all the shots, you won't have a job.

He expected nothing to come out. He went into the knee and a bunch of fluid flew out. I was just happy that here's one big reason the horse ran so bad.

Upon winning the California Derby, Simply Majestic became an overnight Kentucky Derby contender. "I felt all along he was a good horse," John told reporters after that race, "but he had problems back East, and then we shipped him to Florida and he still had problems. He has started coming into his own in California, and after today he has to be one of the Derby favorites."

There was a problem, though, that would prevent Simply Majestic from running in the big race at Churchill Downs, and in the Preakness and Belmont.

"**Oversight Costs Simply Majestic His Derby Run,**" read the headline in the *Los Angeles Times*. "Simply Majestic ... is not eligible to run in the Kentucky Derby or the other two Triple Crown races, apparently the victim of having too many trainers," the story began. It quoted the executive director of Triple Crown Productions, that no one submitted an entry form or paid the nomination fee, and Lukas, saying, "I'm guessing that when the horse was transferred out of my barn, nobody did anything about nominating him. I don't think it was my responsibility by then."

Despite that story and a report in *The New York Times* two days later that stated, "The Majestic Prince colt was not nominated for the Triple Crown because he switched trainers briefly this winter and each thought the other was handling the paperwork," Sabarese says it wasn't a matter of confusion. Another horse that he owned and John trained—named Frank Wright, after the TV commentator—was one of the three hundred sixty-eight Thoroughbreds nominated for the Triple Crown by the January 15 deadline. Simply Majestic was not. Nor was he nominated before the March 17 extended cutoff date, which was met by twenty-four additional entries.

"John's all excited," Sabarese recalled, "and says, 'We gotta run him in the Kentucky Derby.' I said, 'John, I never nominated him for the Kentucky Derby.' Back in those days you could supplement him in but I said, 'I'm not doing that.' It was some crazy number." (The early entry fee was $600; in March it was $3,000—pocket change compared to the price Sabarese had paid to buy the horse as a yearling.)

* * *

A YEAR LATER, IN THE BUDWEISER Breeders' Cup Handicap, Simply Majestic would earn the headline: "Secretariat's World Record for 1 1/8 Miles Broken by Simply Majestic at Golden Gate."

It turned into a match race with a colt named Judge Angelucci, a horse of some renown at the time who was trained by future Hall of Famer Charlie Whittingham. The Judge had beaten 1986 Kentucky Derby winner Ferdinand, the 1987 Horse of The Year, twice in eight months. In June of '87 he won the Californian Stakes at Hollywood Park in 1:48.2, leading wire-to-wire; Ferdinand was fourth. On February 14, 1988, he bested Ferdinand again, this time by three-and-a-half lengths in 1:48.6 in the San Antonio Handicap at Santa Anita. Both races were a mile-and-an-eighth, the same distance as the race at Golden Gate Fields.

Thirty years later Sabarese excitedly recalled Simply Majestic's historic victory as if the race had just been run.

"There were four horses in the race. Judge Angelucci goes off 1-to-5. We break, and Simply Majestic and Judge Angelucci—we were on the outside—go head-to-head.

The fractions were unbelievable: twenty-one and change, :44.2; 1:07.4. I mean, you couldn't even see the other horses in the picture.

"The announcer says, 'They're head-to-head. Simply Majestic has been with him every step of the way. But the Judge has more left; he'll come again.'

"We were in front by just a head. All of a sudden, we come around the turn and we leave him standing still. We broke Secretariat's world record for a mile and an eighth (by two-fifths of a second with a time of 1:45 flat); won the race by 10 lengths.

"The Judge was second and the rest of the horses were so far back you couldn't even see them."

In October 1988, Simply Majestic won the Budweiser Breeders' Cup at Calder with a wire-to-wire burst of speed, beating Val d'Enchere by five and a half lengths and breaking the "about 1" (one hundred twelve feet short of a mile) turf course record by two-fifths with a time of 1:43 3/5. "There was nothing much to do," jockey J.D. Bailey said. "I just sat on him and he did the rest. He did everything on his own. I wasn't surprised nobody came after me because nobody had the speed to do that."

Afterwards, John told the *Fort Lauderdale Sun-Sentinel* racing writer: "This is our Breeders' Cup horse. This is a super horse. I know we'll win the mile race on the grass Nov. 5 in Kentucky. I don't care who's coming from Europe." Alas, on his first trip to the home of The Kentucky Derby, Simply Majestic, with Angel Cordero up, finished third to the defending champion, the French filly Miesque, on a rainswept day.

The literal storm of race day became a figurative one. The tech bubble burst, and Ted Sabarese, founder of the $200 million Ultimate Computer Corporation, was among those hardest hit.

> "Ted is trying to stay afloat," John was quoted in print, "but he's up against it right now in business. Unfortunately, it is the racing stable that has to suffer in the meantime. The stable, as it stands right now, is a luxury that can't be afforded.
>
> "We've won ten stakes races this year and placed in a Breeder' Cup race. The stable has $1.6 million in earnings and it looks like it'll reach $2 million. This is, without a doubt, our best year ever, but it still isn't enough. When you're talking about a stock that falls from thirty-seven to nine, you can see it isn't enough.
>
> "We have two standout horses this year. We have Chapel of Dreams, a Northern Dancer filly who is probably the third or fourth best turf filly in the country. And we have Simply Majestic, who was third in the Breeders' Cup Mile ... Given our position, they're for sale, unfortunately ... everything we have is for sale."

Simply Majestic was never sold, and was retired after running fourteen races in 1989. He finished fifth in his last two races, after winning eight of his previous ten, including three more starts at Golden Gate. He won almost $1.7 million with eighteen firsts, four seconds and seven thirds in forty-four races (65.9%). His world record still stood in 2018.

John's Jockey

ANGEL CORDERO JR. RODE HIS FIRST winner in Puerto Rico on June 15, 1960, when John Parisella was just 19 years old, and came to the U.S. to ride two years later. He won his 5,000th race in 1983, and became only the third jockey in history to ride seven thousand winners on October 17, 1991. His induction into the Horse Racing Hall of Fame at Saratoga occurred in 1988.

As the saying goes, John is one who can say, "I knew him when ..."

The friendship between John and the man called The King of Saratoga began well before John went out on his own as a trainer. "I know John since the late sixties," Cordero said. "I met him when he was a groom for John Campo. Then he became a trainer and I got very lucky in my profession so he started riding me. We became a very good team."

Cordero was anything but the star he would become when John first approached him at Belmont. Not long before, a discouraged Cordero had asked a fellow jockey for a ride to the airport to return to his native Puerto Rico—deciding to stay only after his friend taunted him that going home might be right because "New York is for good riders only." Finding it hard to land mounts, Cordero groomed horses and exercised them in the mornings in exchange for the opportunity to ride them in races. Still, John could see his talent.

> *I went to him and I told him, "I just want you to know that one day hopefully I'll be your trainer. And a good one, hopefully.*
>
> *But you'll always be my favorite jock. I think you're the best jock, and I've watched many races.*

Three and a half years passed before I became a trainer. He rode my first horse. He rode for me a lot.

He's the best ever. If he rode a cheap horse, it meant as much to him as a good horse. I can't say that about another jockey. He'd compliment other trainers when he got beat. He won the Eclipse Award (for top jockey) in his forties. His work ethic was incredible.

One of the times when I was broke, he came by the barn—he was the leading jockey at the time—and he galloped horses for me, which no jockey ever does. That's the relationship we have.

"I call him Papa, and I'm older than him," Cordero said. "Because he's been like a father to me. He's always been on my side. He help me so much in my career—before I became an agent, and after I became an agent. We've been personal friends for a long, long time—with horses, and without horses.

"He's a good horseman because he learned from a good horseman, John Campo. He ran a good ship, very organized. He had good owners who gave him a free hand. He was not only a good trainer; he's a good human being and a great friend."

Cordero's second Preakness victory, on Gate Dancer, illustrates the close relationship between John and the jockey. A 19-1 longshot in the Kentucky Derby, Gate Dancer challenged eventual winner Swale in the stretch at Churchill Downs but finished fourth (ahead of seventh-place Fight Over), and was set back to fifth after stewards upheld a foul claim that Gate Dancer bumped another horse several times. Cordero was not riding Gate Dancer that day, but he replaced that jockey for the Preakness.

"John was training a horse that I was riding for him," Cordero said, "and he was going to the Preakness. I was supposed to ride Fight Over. I won a couple races on him, but had the chance to ride Gate Dancer and it looked like Gate Dancer was going to be one of the favorites. I asked him if I don't ride his horse and ride the other horse instead. He said, 'The other horse is a better horse; go ahead.' Fight Over ran third (five lengths behind Cordero's winning mount). John was pretty good about it."

Cordero won his second Derby two years later with Bold Forbes, and his third in 1985 on another three-year-old with ties to his close friend: Spend a Buck, the horse John wanted to buy at Calder the year before.

* * *

BORN IN SANTURCE, PUERTO RICO, Cordero grew up around Thoroughbreds. His father, Angel Cordero Sr., was a rider and trainer, as were his grandfather and uncles. In America, Cordero Sr. was his son's most vocal critic, and John often intervened.

> *His father was the typical Puerto Rican—little guy, big hat. When his father wanted to yell at him—tell him, "You had a bad ride"—I'd get in the middle and break it up. We hung out together a lot.*

"They were very close," Cordero said. "I didn't realize it until my father passed away. When my father passed, we became very close. John was, for me, there all the time. I have a lot of love for him and a lot of respect."

Cordero was a regular at Saratoga, one of John's favorite tracks. And just as John was named "Trainer to the Stars," Cordero became known as "The King of Saratoga." He was the leading rider there fourteen times, including eleven years in a row. But such success didn't come easily or quickly.

"The King" once left Saratoga Springs on a bus, unable to land enough mounts. He said he borrowed $25 every week to pay his share of the rent on a two-bedroom apartment he was sharing with two other riders. One of them got a bed for doing the cooking, he said, so Cordero and his other roommate flipped a coin to see who slept on the floor.

By his own count, Cordero was involved in twenty-four spills and was hospitalized eighteen times. John was there for him in 1978 when he suffered a broken back at Hollywood Park.

I'm training in California, and one day Angel took one of the worst spills. I'll never forget the name of horse because it was almost a tragedy: Black Hills.

They recommended doctors to him. I said, "Angel, let me take care of it. My uncle will know the very best doctor for you."

And where other people had told him it would be so long, he went to my uncle's doctor and he cut the time in half.

"I compressed the sixth, seventh, eighth, ninth and tenth vertebrae," Cordero recalled. "The doctors said I would be out three months. John recommended a doctor that he knew. I went to see him and I was back riding in a month."

That's what Cordero remembered and appreciated most about John.

"Whenever I got hurt, he always tried to contact me with the best doctors," Cordero said. "Whenever I needed some legal advice, he always connected me with the best lawyers he knew. He had great connections. If you need something, a big favor to meet somebody or get to somebody, if he don't know the person, he'll find somebody who does."

Cordero rode Simply Majestic several times, including once at Golden Gate Fields where Simply Majestic was unbeaten and had broken Secretariat's world-record time in the mile-and-an-eighth. Defending his title in the Budweiser Breeders Cup Handicap in April 1989, Simply Majestic won by seven lengths. A photo in the next day's *San Francisco Chronicle* showed Cordero, so far ahead of the field, turning and looking back as he approached the wire. **"Majestic Romp at GGF,"** read the headline.

> *Golden Gate was a very small track compared to Santa Anita or Hollywood. Cordero wouldn't normally ride there. But I said to him, "You have to come up to Golden Gate and ride Simply Majestic for me; our friendship's on the line. And he came! He wouldn't have done that for anyone else.*

* * *

CORDERO RELUCTANTLY ENDED HIS CAREER as a jockey following a life-threatening, four-horse spill at Aqueduct in January 1992. He broke three ribs and his left arm when he was thrown into a strut supporting the inner rail, and subsequently underwent surgery to remove his spleen. Though he returned to ride in the 1995 Breeders' Cup ("I want to retire my way, not the other way," he said then), Cordero effectively retired following the 1992 accident.

"Margie didn't want me to ride anymore," he said of his wife when he retired, "because she was afraid something was going to happen to me. When I quit riding, it was the biggest pain I went through except when my father died, because it's all I wanted to do in life. That's when I knew she was more important than anything else in life, because I never would have stopped riding for anybody else."

Cordero tried his hand as a trainer then became the agent for John Velazquez, who became so successful that he was inducted into the Horse Racing Hall of Fame when he was only forty-one years old, and set the record for purse-winnings by a jockey two years later with more than three hundred million dollars.

> *Angel's wife, Marjorie Clayton, once wrote in* The Daily Racing Form *that if she ever came back to exercising horses, she would take only one job, and that was with me. She came*

to me and said, "We're having a hard time training. Please tell Angel to take Velazquez's book."

So I went to him with another trainer, and I said to him: "Angel, training—it's not working out. You and Margie shouldn't have all that pressure. You can make all kinds of money with Velazquez."

As Cordero told it, the message was much more blunt. "He said, 'You better take this kid. If you don't, I'm going to kick your ass.' So I finally decided to do it, and I'm glad I did."

Marjorie Clayton Cordero was Angel's second wife. They met in 1983, around the time Marjorie, also a jockey then, won her first race astride a horse named Solandra at Keystone in Pennsylvania.

He was wild then, he admitted—married but not home much and not caring about much except riding horses. Bluntly telling him if she ever caught him cheating, she'd leave, Margie became his best friend and soul mate. They were often seen on the backside holding hands and kissing. Eventually Angel married her, and they became the parents of two daughters and a son.

An unexpected tragedy ended their love story the night of January 22, 2001 when a black Ford struck Marjorie from behind as she crossed a busy road in the small Long Island town of Greenvale, just a few hundred yards from her home.

"When it happened," Cordero said, "it hit me very hard. I isolated myself; didn't want to be around too many people. John reached for me. He was there; told me he'd do whatever he could do. But in a situation like that there isn't much anybody can do when you lose somebody that you're very close to. But he was there for support.

"I love the man like he was my father. I have a lot of love for him, and a lot of respect."

Far Turn

Previous page: Photo with inscription by Rick Pitino; Gabrielle in the arms of her mom, Melissa Sanders; John with his baby daughter *(photos courtesy of John Parisella)*

NBA Insider

A LOT WAS HAPPENING IN JOHN PARISELLA'S life besides the collapse of Ted Sabarese's financial empire during the last half of the 1980s. Joe Pepitone was arrested and John interceded on his behalf with George Steinbrenner... Spend a Buck won The Derby... Simply Majestic won eighteen starts in four years and broke a world record set by Secretariat... Bethenny turned sixteen then graduated from high school then went off to college, beginning what would become a spectacular business and entertainment career—without John in her life... Mafioso Paul Castellano and his driver/bodyguard—John's "Italian cousin" (i.e. a family friend)—were murdered in a mob hit in front of New York City's Sparks Steak House—the last mobster killed in public until Francesco "Frankie Boy" Cali was gunned down in March 2019...

... And John became close friends with Rick Pitino.

That last event marked a turning point in John's career and life. "He's like the brother I never had," John has said. "When I was down, he kept picking me up both in person and over the phone."

A 2013 inductee into the Naismith Memorial Basketball Hall of Fame, Rick Pitino is one of only two coaches to have led two different college programs to at least three Final Fours each; is one of only four coaches to have taken a school to the Final Four in four separate decades; and is the only coach to lead three schools (Providence, Kentucky and Louisville) to a Final Four. Only one other coach has won national championships with two universities.

A couple months before the 2017-18 season began Pitino became the FBI's poster boy in its attempt to crack down on shoe companies influencing the recruitment of top high school basketball players, and lost his job as head coach at the University of Louisville when he was implicated, though not explicitly named. A year later he hadn't been charged with any crime. Adding to the ignominy, he became the only men's basketball coach in NCAA history to have a national championship vacated. In September 2018 he published a book, *PITINO: My Story*, that tells his side of the dubious affair.

John and Rick met while Pitino was head coach at Providence. After winning eleven and losing twenty in 1984-85, the Friars improved to 17-14 in Pitino's first season. He had been hired at Providence after five seasons at Boston University, where he won two league championships and coached the Terriers to the NCAA Tournament for the first time in twenty-four years while compiling a 91-51 record. The matchmaker who brought John and Rick together was Joe Taub, founder of the data processing giant ADP and principal owner of the New Jersey Nets. Taub had a reputation for trying to recruit big-name coaches, and was an owner and breeder of Thoroughbreds. John was his trainer at one time.

> *Joe Taub was a bottom-line guy. You had to be a proven factor with him. He knew how great Rick did at Boston U.*
>
> *Taub was trying to interest Rick in coaching the Nets. It was his money that got Frank Lautenberg elected to the U.S. Senate. He brought Rick to meet me because he thought it would impress Rick. He knew Rick liked the horses.*
>
> *We hit it off, made plans to see each other again. I introduced him to racing. We really grew fond of each other out of nowhere.*
>
> *He gave me the nickname "Horse." He made all the players call me that.*

"He named several of his horses after my teams," Pitino said. "It was Friar Magic, Backcourt Press ... things like that. I had a couple horses with him. The big race I won was the Bed of Roses at Aqueduct. We won a race, then he ran him five days later and he won the Bed of Roses. It was shocking."

Pitino's horses won frequently when John trained them. Testament to both that success and their close relationship is one of the commemorative prints that horse tracks provided after races: the finish line photo showing the winning mount ahead of the field, and a Winner's Circle shot imprinted with the name of the track, name of the race, date, winning horse and time, and names of the owner, jockey and trainer.

From Golden Gate Fields near San Francisco, dated 3/11/89, the top half shows a horse named Pitino Ball all alone at the finish of a six-furlong race, its winning time 1:11.4. Handwritten on the lower half, which shows John, jockey Ron Hansen astride the horse, and others in a line abreast, is:

> To Horse,
>
> It's great to have the #1 trainer behind your horse! Thanks for your loyalty and friendship.
>
> Rick

"With John, everybody gets a nickname," Pitino said during an interview at Saratoga in 2018, citing a few examples: *Clipboard ... Calamari ... Cueball.* "I think I'm one of his few friends who doesn't have a nickname."

* * *

TAUB ENVISIONED PITINO SUCCEEDING DAVE WOHL, who went 39-43 and finished seventh the previous year. Wohl had not yet been fired but would have been shown the door if Taub had succeeded in luring Pitino. But Pitino declined, instead taking Providence to the Final Four in 1987 behind a spunky guard named Billy Donovan, then becoming head coach of the rival New York Knicks. Overnight, John Parisella became a National Basketball Association insider and intermediary between the coach and his boss, General Manager Al Bianchi, who was hired five days before Pitino but had no say in choosing the next Knicks coach.

"I didn't get along with the general manager from a basketball standpoint," Pitino said. "Off the court, he liked horses; I liked horses. Socially, he was fine; we were fine. On the court, I wanted to play fast; he wanted to play slow. He wanted to play like the Pistons; I wanted to play like the Lakers.

"So anytime I had a problem with something I wanted him to do, I'd send John. They got along great together. Al loved the horses, and John was a Damon Runyon character who loved the horses. John was the ambassador: 'Go to him and get it done.'"

I started attending all the home games, and we had a ritual where Rick would stop by my seat and shake hands, and I would wish him luck.

A native New Yorker like John and Pitino, Bianchi played ten seasons in the NBA with the Syracuse Nationals and Philadelphia Warriors (after the Nats relocated before the 1963-64 season). One of the last players to use the two-handed set shot, he averaged 8.1 points per game for his career. He coached the expansion Seattle Supersonics in the NBA for two years, and the Washington Caps/Virginia Squires of the American Basketball Association for six seasons. He's a member of the New York City and Ohio Basketball Halls of Fame. (He played collegiately at Bowling Green.)

Of the numerous examples of John's work with Bianchi on Pitino's behalf, none better illustrates it than the tale of Donovan, that spunky guard from Pitino's Final Four Providence team. Billy thought of transferring when Pitino became head coach, concerned that he wasn't good enough to play for him. Instead, he became captain of the Friars' NCAA Tournament team by working hard at every grueling drill Pitino prescribed. He played in forty-four games for Pitino's first Knicks team after signing as a free agent two weeks before Christmas. His career ended the following March.

> *I get a phone call at twenty 'til eleven, and Pitino says, "Look, they got this guy coming in to replace Billy Donovan. And the Big East (Tournament) is starting. It will really hurt him. You have to talk to Bianchi."*
>
> *I said, "Are you crazy?" Naturally, Rick had no shot because Bianchi hated his guts.*
>
> *"And you can't mention my name," he says.*
>
> *I tell a friend next to me, and he says, "What, are you nuts, John!? You can't do that. The guy goes to bed at eight o'clock."*
>
> *I wake Bianchi up. I say, "Al." He goes, "John, what's wrong? What's wrong?"*
>
> *I say, "Al, I never asked for anything. You're the one who's been so good to me. Al, let me tell you something. You know Billy Donovan. There's not a nicer kid on the planet."*
>
> *He says, "Yeah, yeah, John, what's the matter?"*
>
> *I say, "You're going to let him go tomorrow. You can't do that."*
>
> *"John, we're all ready to sign Sedric Toney tomorrow."*
>
> *I say, "Al, this is one of the nicest kids on the planet. His father, his grandfather, are two of the finest human beings. They come in the paddock and everything. You're not that*

kind of person to hurt somebody in that family. You're not made that way. And for me to be calling you at this time to wake you, because I know you need your ... beauty sleep ... you know how important this is to me.

He says, "What do I do with Toney?"

I say, "Let him wash cars or something. As long as you give him money, I don't care. I just want Billy there for the Big East. Day after that, let him go. As long as he's there while the Big East Tournament's going on."

And he did.

The 1988 Big East Tournament was played at Madison Square Garden March 10-13, with Syracuse defeating Villanova 85-68 in the championship game. Sedric Toney was signed by the Knicks on March 13, and Billy Donovan was waived March 28. (Five days later Simply Majestic broke Secretariat's world record at Golden Gate Fields.)

The Knicks, who finished 24-58 the previous season, were the eighth and final team to make the Eastern Conference playoffs, finishing 38-44 in Pitino's first season as head coach. Donovan became a college coach and went on to win two national championships and record sixteen straight 20-win seasons in nineteen years as the University of Florida's head coach. (In 2015 he returned to the NBA as head coach of the Oklahoma City Thunder.)

I don't think Rick ever told him. Three years later, I saw him when he was scouting a high-school player. I called to him and he ran into the stands and hugged me. He said, "I can't wait to tell my father I saw you! I can't wait!"

As head coach of New York's pro basketball team, Rick Pitino was a Big Apple celebrity early in his coaching career. Not yet thirty-seven nor wise in the ways of the world when the Knicks hired him, he benefitted from John's intervention off the court, too, as evidenced by an experience with the businessman who partnered with a childhood friend to establish the multibillion-dollar Calvin Klein clothing line.

> *Rick would shake hands with me before every game. Barry Schwartz, who put up the money to get Calvin Klein started, said, "John, will you do me a favor? I'll have my son sitting close by. Would you have Coach Pitino shake hands with him?"*
>
> *I said, "Sure, Barry."*
>
> *Later, Rick tells me, "Wow, Barry invited me up to pick out four or five suits."*
>
> *I said, "Rick, listen to me. Don't go up there. I'm telling you now."*
>
> *He said, "Whaddya mean?"*
>
> *I said, "I'm telling you. I know Barry Schwartz."*
>
> *Rick says no, he told me this and that.*
>
> *So many times we had this conversation. I finally said, "Do what the --- you want."*
>
> *So sure enough, Rick says, "Why not, I'm going up and get those Armani suits." He gets five suits, this, that. He told me, "John, pick something." I didn't pick anything.*
>
> *About a month and a half later, I'm at Aqueduct and I get a phone call. Rick was livid. "John, you have to take care of this."*
>
> *"What now?"*
>
> *"I just got a bill for twenty thousand from Barry Schwartz."*

I said, "No. I'm not going to do it. Because you're the one who wouldn't listen to me. I told you ..." And I hung the phone up.

Like four seconds later, the phone's ringing again. I have to pick it up, naturally. I said, "No. I told you not to go," and I hung up again. We had that kind of relationship. Unbelievable friendship.

The phone rings again. I said, "What is it? Please. I'm sick to my stomach. I have a migraine. You didn't listen to me. I know people. You know the decision I made. I begged you not to go there. And you want me to get on the phone and tell the guy to forget the twenty thousand."

He says, "Yeah, that's what you gotta do."

I said, "Look, I don't give --- about Barry Schwartz. So you got that going for you." I didn't respect the guy. Not a bad guy, but not my kind of guy. Egomaniac. He and his wife are high-rollers.

"I told you I don't like the guy, and I don't trust him. But I'm going to call. But you know what? You're not going to learn a --- lesson, and I don't know if I can get you out of twenty thousand dollars. Maybe I can get it reduced."

He says, 'I ain't paying a --- penny."

I said, "You're not even going for a reduction?"

"I ain't paying a --- penny."

In addition to his role as Chief Executive Officer of Calvin Klein, Barry Schwartz had a distinguished career in horse racing. Beginning in 1979 he owned Stonewall Farm, a 750-acre horse farm; from 2000 to 2004 he was chairman of the New York Racing Association; and he received the New York Turf Writers' 2001 Alfred Vanderbilt Award as the person who did the most for racing.

> *I'm smart enough that I ain't doing it on the phone. I'm waiting to see him in person, because he was coming to the track.*
>
> *I said, "Barry, listen to me. You're very rich. Forget that you're making me look bad. That doesn't mean anything. But you're making yourself look bad. Because I'm telling you point-blank, I'll let everyone know what happened."*
>
> *"What are you talking about, John?" He gets nervous. It scared him.*
>
> *I said, "You've got the --- balls. After you tell Rick, 'Come pick anything you want,' you send him a bill for twenty thousand!" And he looked at me.*
>
> *I said, "You're not getting a --- penny. Do you understand that? And don't let me make any --- phone calls." He knows my background.*
>
> *"I'm going to tell the whole racetrack, that you told him to come up and get this for nothing. You're not getting a penny. You understand that?*
>
> *"And you send him a --- letter: 'You don't owe me anything.'"*
>
> *He sent the --- letter.*
>
> *So now Rick gets on the phone. I said, "--- you," and I hung the phone up.*

One might reasonably assume John burned a bridge with Barry Schwartz with such a blunt confrontation. But what followed suggests otherwise.

Barry Schwartz has a stable, and is well-known. He's splitting up with his trainer. I met with him and his wife. They wanted me to become their trainer.

I turned them down and stayed with Sabarese—with three horses. They were dumbfounded. But I had a relationship with Ted.

* * *

A FEW WEEKS BEFORE PITINO was hired as the Knicks' head coach they had made Mark Jackson, a guard from John's alma mater, their first-round draft pick. Jackson averaged double figures in points and assists as a rookie, and made the NBA All-Star team the next season. John became one of Jackson's close friends and played a role in landing a player who helped make the Knicks division champions in Pitino's and Jackson's second year: Charles Oakley.

Mark Jackson played good basketball because of Rick Pitino. Rick said to him—kept drilling it into him: "You're the best guard in the league." Drilled it into him, time and time again.

Mark loved me. When they couldn't get things done with him, they came to me. One time they wanted him to go on the Roy Firestone Show. He wouldn't go. The CEO of Gulf & Western, which owned the Knicks, came to me and said "John, we know you have a special relationship. It really will be important to the organization if you could get him to go on."

I said, "I can't guarantee it. I know you're part of this; you're Rick's boss, and because of that, I'll try. I feel awkward, but I'll try."

And I got him to go. Mark Jackson is a beautiful person. I just don't think he was ready to exploit himself then.

The Knicks acquired Oakley in a trade with the Chicago Bulls the day before the 1988 NBA draft. The teams swapped first and third-round draft choices, and the Knicks gave up seven-foot-one center Bill Cartwright.

> *I'm with Rick one day—we were taking a day trip to Providence to visit friends—and Bianchi calls with a possible trade with the Bulls: Cartwright for Charles Oakley. Rick says, "Let me think about it. I'll get back to you."*
>
> *He told me about it, and I said, "Are you crazy? Do it!"*
>
> *He called Bianchi back.*

Despite John's gregarious nature and his friendship with Jackson and eventually Oakley, it took a year for John to get Patrick Ewing to warm up to him. Ewing had been subjected to racial taunts and jeers as a high school star. Once, rival fans even rocked his team's bus upon arrival for a road game.

> *Because of what he went through in high school, with racism, he found it very difficult to deal with white people. The first year around him I had no interaction. I would say hello and he would just nod his head.*
>
> *The second year, I am not sure if Mark talked to him, but Patrick started opening up to me. We became great friends. To hear about his experiences with racism, I can understand why he avoided talking to me.*

John was serving a 60-day suspension imposed by stewards at Belmont during part of the 1988-89 NBA season, so he became an almost constant presence with the Knicks—in the locker room and on the bench. Pitino told him: "No gambling, John. That's the only thing I'm asking you. Otherwise, if you want to gamble, you're a great friend to me and I understand gambling, but I can't let you in the locker room." So, John said, he never gambled when he was around the Knicks. "He'd go to every home game," Pitino said "We'd meet at the New York Athletic Club. He traveled with the team a few times."

It was during a road trip to Los Angeles that John crossed a line and had to be reeled in. "We were in The Forum in L.A., and Oakley got into a fight," Pitino recalled. "I'm in the middle of it. The benches have cleared. And who's on the floor but John Parisella, making sure I'm okay. That's when Al said, "We have to keep John off the floor. He can't ever go on the floor."

> Bianchi calls me in and says, "John, you can't do that. Please, you can't do something like that." I was worried about Rick—not that I'm a tough guy, but I ran to his defense. I pushed him away.

Another time when the Knicks were in Los Angeles that year, John drew the ire of the coach himself.

> We're in LA and I had a Porsche. I had some horses there. So I gave Oakley and Mark Jackson my Porsche.

> They were out all night and didn't come back until the next day, and missed practice. Rick came screaming into the room, "What the --- are you doing? You give those guys a --- Porsche to run around in!"

> I loved it. And they loved me, because I took it on the chin. It was all me. I convinced them to ride in the car. So they loved me even more.

Oakley and Jackson led the team as New York improved to 52-30 and won the Atlantic Division of the Eastern Conference in the 1988-89 season. (The Knicks won their first-round series against Philadelphia, and

John led the team in a rousing rendition of the Sinatra song *New York! New York!* on the bus ride after the clinching game.) Oakley played with the Knicks for ten years, setting a record in 1994 by starting all eighty-two games in the regular season and all twenty-five playoff games the Knicks played. He was a first-team all-NBA defender that year, and an NBA All-Star. He and Jackson would end their long NBA careers as Houston Rockets teammates in the 2003-04 season.

* * *

JOHN'S ROLE AS INTERMEDIARY BETWEEN Pitino and Bianchi wasn't limited to player matters. Going into his second season as head coach, Pitino had an assistant coach vacancy to fill. It was John's job to convince Bianchi that Ralph Willard should be the choice. Willard had been an assistant under Jim Boeheim at Syracuse when the Orange beat Pitino's Providence Friars in the Final Four semifinals in 1987. He came to the Knicks when Pitino was named head coach, though not in a coaching role.

> *Rick got him a job with the Knicks, but it was like, filing papers or something. He says, "I gotta make him an assistant coach."*
>
> *I said, "How are you going to do that? Bianchi hates your guts, and Ralph's your friend and Al knows that. How you gonna do that?"*
>
> *He says, "You're going to do it."*
>
> *I said, "Are you nuts? Bianchi knows that you and Ralph are close friends, and I'm going to ask Al to make him your assistant? I can't do that."*
>
> *He says, "I'm asking you."*

"You love Ralph," he tells me. I shook my head.

John first approached Bianchi head-on.

We're sitting in a restaurant and I say, "Al, I want to talk to you about something." He knows right away.

"Okay, John, what is it?"

"I'm giving you great advice. Do you believe in our friendship?"

He said yes.

"Then please believe, this will help you big time with Pitino. Big, big time."

"Okay. What is it?"

"Assistant coach position is available. I think it should be Ralph Willard in the job."

He says, "John, I mean, really? What are you, nuts? They're best friends. And I don't like the other guy. You know that. How could I do that?"

"You don't understand. He's a calming factor for Rick. So if you want to get some things done with Rick, which I know I can't do because we fight all the time and everything, Ralph is a calming factor to him. It'll be a better aid for you with Pitino to have him as a liaison than even me. And Ralph Willard is first-class, trustworthy, and he'll never ever go behind your back. I swear on all that's holy."

John felt he had given it his best shot and Bianchi had rejected the idea. He went back to Pitino with the bad news.

I told Rick, "I pitched it to him. I wasn't successful. I tried."

> He said, "Keep working at it. You'll find a way to get it done."

John used their common love of horse racing to create the right environment for approaching Bianchi again.

> Bianchi was a two-dollar bettor; not a gambler, but he loved it. I was running in a stakes race in L.A., Santa Anita. I had to go out there two days before. I put Ralph on Sabarese's plane, the big one, along with Bianchi and some of his friends.
>
> I told Ralph, "Rick's put me in a position here, I honestly don't think I can do this. But I'm trying."
>
> Ralph said, "John I know you can't do this. I'm sorry Rick asked you."
>
> I said, "Talk to the guy."
>
> I'm a gambler. I would have bet against myself in this spot. I knew I had a shot with Billy Donovan. But I felt I had no shot here. The one thing I had going for me was that Ralph's an exceptionally nice guy.
>
> They interact. It's very easy for Ralph to talk because Bianchi doesn't have any idea what I'm planning.

Willard and Bianchi spent time together on the plane, as John intended, as well as at the racetrack and later at dinner. On the flight back to New York, Bianchi surprised John.

> He comes to me and he says, "Ralph seems to be the guy you made him out to be, and a person I can trust. I am willing to take a chance against my better judgment and hire him. I hope it works out."
>
> It did.

Pitino would leave the Knicks at the end of the '88-'89 season, and Willard would follow him to Kentucky. Later Willard became a college head coach, first at Western Kentucky then Pittsburgh and Holy Cross, before reuniting with Pitino at Louisville. As he did so often with the Knicks, John played a key role in Pitino's move to Lexington.

"He waffled on that," Pitino said of John. "At first it was, 'You can't leave the Knicks. You can't leave the Knicks. You can't go to those hardboots.' Then he started putting it together."

Bianchi's 'Beard'

EVERY COUPLE HAS A STORY ABOUT how they met. John Parisella and Melissa Sanders are no exception. It happened at a pro basketball game between the Golden State Warriors and the New York Knicks, coached by Rick Pitino, in February 1988. The Knicks won 125-119. The Billy Donovan-Big East Tournament saga was still a couple weeks away, but already John was into his relationship with New York general manager Al Bianchi.

"I met John in 1988," Melissa said. "It was in the Bay Area, Oakland. I think he flew out on the plane with Rick. I was coming out of a divorce."

> *I wasn't traveling with Rick. The purpose of that trip was Bianchi. Bianchi had a girlfriend and he needed me to be his beard. You know, "The broad is with me."*
>
> *His girlfriend was Melissa's boss. She brought Melissa along. You know, "C'mon, I'll take you to the game." She didn't know anything about me being there.*
>
> *There's myself, Bianchi's girlfriend and Melissa. That's how we met.*

A native of Washington state who graduated from the University of Washington, Melissa Sanders grew up around horses, though not around horse racing or racetracks. The lone daughter in a family with three sons, she developed the independence and resourcefulness borne of having three older brothers. For much of her adult life she worked in marketing, design and public relations, mostly from home as a working mom running her own business. She moved to northern California in 1985.

John was almost twenty years older than Melissa, but a lasting relationship developed over the remainder of 1988. Without stating why, he told a *San Francisco Chronicle* writer he made twenty-eight cross-country flights that year alone. "John and I became friends," Melissa said. "We've just always been really close friends. He's got the heart of Texas and the brain of a rocket scientist, and the personality of a crazy person. But to know him is to love him. He's a really interesting combination of a lot of different things."

Bianchi saw what was happening and admonished John.

As Melissa and I became close, Bianchi said to me: "You better be careful. Don't put this on me, that I introduced you."

Melissa had been married to former pro football player Mike Keller before she and John met. Her son Sam was four when the marriage ended.

"Divorce can be traumatizing, for the adults and for the children," she said. "John was my port in the storm. He helped me so much during that time. He embraced my four-year-old son and helped us through it all."

Sam Keller became a football player, too, a quarterback who played three seasons at Arizona State and one at Nebraska. In his sophomore season at ASU he made his first collegiate start against Purdue in the Sun Bowl. He passed for 370 yards and three touchdowns in a comeback victory that earned him the Sun Bowl Most Valuable Player Award.

"It was a tough time," Sam said, "being a youngster but being old enough to kind of understand: My mom and my dad weren't going to be together anymore."

Gabrielle was born in August the year after John and Melissa met, and it changed John forever.

When my daughter was born, I threw drugs out the window. No rehab. Prayed hard. If she wasn't born, I'm living a wild life.

Melissa wasn't willing to come to New York (to live), but that's where I had all my horses. I didn't have any clients in California at that time.

I really believed she would be a good mom. Turned out she's a great mom.

John's close friendship with Rick Pitino reached a new level when John asked him to be Gabby's godfather. The coach was honored, and Melissa was fine with it.

"Rick and John were close friends," she said. "Rick was the most normal man. To me, it didn't really matter a whole lot. I was going to raise my daughter the way I was going to raise my daughter. So whoever was godfather didn't really matter. When we were at her baptism, he was genuinely present, and wonderful all throughout."

Pitino, in fact, proved to be more than the prototypical godfather by religious standards, Melissa said.

"Rick's been amazing. We didn't need him, quote-unquote, for anything, but he's always been there. He's taken care of his relationship with his goddaughter, and Gabby will tell you that. They have a nice relationship. They've done things on their own together. He's sent her gifts on his own—team logo things, sweats every year. He's a very special person."

Baby Gabrielle's first year was an eventful one, though only her mother and father remember the details. She went to her first Kentucky Derby when she was nine months old in 1990—the year John had to scratch sore-footed Country Day—then was hospitalized with a dangerously high fever and swollen lymph node just weeks later. John was training in New York when Melissa called to tell him their daughter was very ill.

"I told John what was going on," Melissa said. "We've always kept in close communication. He was upset and I was upset. He dropped everything and jumped on a red-eye. He arrived the next morning from New York. He understood it was an emergency situation. It speaks to his character as a dad."

> *That plane ride was the longest, and I experienced the biggest nightmare, of my life. This wasn't just somebody getting sick. This was going and knowing that they didn't know what was wrong with her. They never knew. That made it worse.*
>
> *So I got to the hospital, and there were two kids who lost their parents in a car accident. Melissa says to me, "Why don't we take care of the two kids." I said, "Let me check and make sure there's no other family." Fortunately, they had a close aunt and uncle to take care of them.*

"It was just really difficult to see your kid in the hospital," Melissa said. "We experienced a horrible day or two then I told the doctors, 'We're leaving.' We got a heavy-duty dose of antibiotics. She had a swollen gland the size of a golf ball, and the regular antibiotics they usually give children weren't cutting it. So we had her on an I-V. At home she got better almost immediately."

> *This was the most difficult decision of my life. She says to me, "John, these doctors aren't getting her better. Our little girl isn't getting any better. I want to take her home."*
>
> *What do I do? Everything's going through my mind. I guess God was on my side. I made the decision to go with her mom.*
>
> *So what I had to do was sign a paper releasing the doctors*

and the hospital of their obligations because I was taking her home against their advice.

She got home, and she got better.

John envisioned a traditional family setting and, with the help of Ken Dunn, bought a "million-dollar house" in the Long Island town of Mill Neck that was anything but your "typical" million-dollar house. This one had been the inanimate co-star with Tom Hanks and Shelley Long in *The Money Pit,* a very funny movie in which the couple sinks a fortune into trying to fix a million-dollar house that is falling apart. It was an ironic abode for John to buy after his experiences with the distressed house he sold to Howard Stern years earlier.

"I'm living in Florida," Dunn recalled. "He's desperate. He wants to impress the mother of his beloved daughter. He wants to buy a house near Belmont. He said, 'I promise to make every payment.' He's living in that house, and she decides she's going to go back to California."

Melissa wasn't willing to come to New York. That's where I had all my horses. So I saw Gabby every six weeks.

I remember being there during the holiday season, in this million-dollar house, sitting on the floor. I was really depressed.

Rick came from seeing his mom on Long Island. He made sure he came by because I didn't answer the phone. It was the morning of Christmas Eve.

He put me on his plane and flew me to his home, to look after me. That Christmas Day the family and I went to see a movie in Lexington. I spent a couple weeks with them.

After Melissa declared her intention to raise Gabby in California, John again enlisted Dunn to buy yet another house. "I get a call," Dunn said. "He says, 'I want to buy a house in Walnut Creek. Would you apply for a mortgage for me?' I have trouble saying 'no' to this guy. I tell him, 'I've got a mortgage in Florida. I've got a mortgage in New York.' He says, 'Call this agent.'

"I call, and I hear the William Tell Overture. Then a voice comes on the line that says, in a French accent, 'Hello! This is Jean. I'm The Loan Arranger.'"

> *I don't want to let go of the property in New York because I know in another year or two I'm going to make money on it, which will be money I need.*
>
> *Ken said, "John, I can't put a third house under my name. Credit-wise, they're not going to approve it." Ken said, "Go and try, but I know on this one, I'm only going to wind up with two houses under my name."*
>
> *I go with Gabby's mom, and I say to this guy, "Jean, look, I have no credit. I have property which is worth money, but I don't want to sell right now. They're under the name of a person who has great credit, but there's no way you can get another mortgage for a third house for him. It's impossible."*
>
> *He tells me, "There's a reason they call me 'The Lone Arranger." He got it done. I wound up with a beautiful house in Walnut Creek. Ken Dunn was in shock.*

* * *

SAM KELLER HAS VIVID MEMORIES of traveling to New York with his mom and baby sister to visit "this strange man."

"I remember being really young, getting dressed as a young kid—living with my mom, a single mom ... getting up early and getting in a limo and going to the airport ... hopping on a TWA flight, when that still existed, and getting off the airplane at JFK or LaGuardia, whatever it was ... and coming down the stairs and seeing a limo driver holding a card with our name on it ...

"Every dinner was really big and over the top," Sam continued. "Everything we did had a little extra oomph to it because that's the man he was. I remember him just being one of the most generous men I've ever met. He took care of people. It was just his deeply rooted Italian ways—how he was raised, how he grew up and where he grew up, what makes his fabric."

Gabby at first was too young to enjoy life on the backside, but her brother wasn't. He has memories that he says will never leave him.

"As a younger kid," Sam said, "I remember getting into the horses because I had to figure out something to occupy my mind. As a youngster I was fascinated with the horses. I'd get up and I'd go with him to the barn, and be up at 5 a.m. every day.

"He'd have Dunkin' Donuts, and Dunkin' Donuts coffee would always be his thing. Remember when Gatorade came in glass bottles? His fridge was always stocked full of those. I would have them from time to time. He always had them on hand.

"It was still dark when we'd go over to the barn," Sam recalled, "and he'd have his horses doing their thing. All the grooms would be out there walking them and doing this and that. He'd go do his thing; I'd go around to every stall and check out every horse. Some of them were mean, and some of them were great. I was just fascinated with that part of it.

"I collected whips from the jockeys. I tried to collect as many whips as I could. That's where my attention was."

Gabby wound up with Roxy, a miniature horse. She would ride around the backside in a cart with Angel Cordero and his daughters.

"Roxy was a miniature pony that John had for, boy, a quarter of a century, I think," recalled Melissa. "Roxy was this adorable little thing that was like having a dog in the barn. John always kept it at his barn, at Aqueduct or Belmont or Florida, or wherever he was. At Saratoga, Gabby would take Roxy out to eat the grass."

> *It was Gabby's birthday, and Angel Cordero's wife, Marjorie Clayton, who I was very close with, had miniature ponies. I said, "I'd really like to get one for my daughter for her birthday." She said, "Oh, John, that would be great."*

> *She told me where to go, so I went out with my daughter. She was so excited—she was going to have her own horse. There were fifty of them, at least, running around. I said, "Okay, Gabs, pick your winner." She said, "This is the one I want, Daddy."*

> *Roxy was part of the family. When I pulled up to my barn, before I even got out of the car, Roxy would come running up.*

That wasn't the only unusual gift in Gabby's childhood. There was also the dollhouse that John A. Gotti sent from G. Williker's in Saratoga Springs. It's a long story that begins with John Parisella's probation and fine for using turn-down shoes in a race at Aqueduct in February 1995. (Turn-downs are horseshoes bent toward the ground at a 45-degree angle at the open-ended rear of the shoe to provide horses with better traction on sandy or cupped tracks. They were banned at New York tracks in 1993.)

> "If I had to do it over again ... well, I'm a horseman and it wasn't like I used a drug or something," John was quoted in a New York newspaper after the trainer of the second-place finisher in the race reported John to track stewards. Contending that he needed the shoes because of the bad track conditions, he added: "I know I violated a rule ... I'm a competitor and I'm not ashamed of what I did."

John A. Gotti, the son of the man they called "The Teflon Don," mob boss John Gotti Jr., saw John's comments and was impressed with John's sense of honor.

> *The owner of my horse was Gotti's friend, and Gotti happened to be good friends with the trainer who made the complaint. That trainer respected Gotti enough to give back the purse money plus the fine.*
>
> *He calls me—this is my only phone call from him—and I said, "Thank you, I really appreciate it." He says, "and another thing is, they told me they looked to call the blacksmith in, and you said, 'It was all my doing.' You're my kind of people. If you ever need anything, I'll be there for you."*
>
> *I wound up going to a charity event that he had.*

Fast-forward to the summer meeting at Saratoga. John's horses went two-for-twenty between July 21 and August 27, winning the second time that last day. But John A. Gotti made the meet a success in an unexpected way.

> *I became friendly with his brother-in-law because his brother-in-law was involved in horse racing. They had a problem with their kids in school, and I got a doctor to write a note that really helped them. And he was really appreciative.*
>
> *We're walking through town; the doctor was with us, who helped him with the children. We walk into this fancy clothing store and Gotti says, "Okay, you guys, pick out whatever you want, because I wouldn't take any money from him. Doctors being doctors, he went ahead and picked out a couple of suits. I said, "No, thank you, that's okay." He became very agitated and I said, "No, its fine."*

We walk around some more, and I said, "Well, let me walk in here (G. Williker's). Maybe I'll find something for my daughter." So we walked in there, and I was looking at things and I saw this beautiful dollhouse. Then I looked at the price and it was a thousand dollars, and I said, "Nah, I gotta find something else."

All of a sudden I looked, and they're packing up the dollhouse and he's asking for my daughter's address. He paid the thousand dollars.

Out in California, Melissa was caught off guard and unnerved when it arrived.

"I opened it up," she recalled, "and it was so grand and so extreme and so over the top, I just said, 'Okay, let's set this thing up.' You had to have half a room. It had everything. It was amazing. I put it up in the playroom and Gabby played with it.

"It was so over the top, I called John and said, 'Okay, obviously somebody found the greatest doll house they could find in the world. That's really great. It's all set up.

"John told me who bought it. I said, 'Oh, great. Thanks. I hope you don't owe him anything. What do we owe him?' I thought, 'God, what am I doing? Why am I having this dollhouse for my daughter?' But she was so young, she didn't understand. She had fun with it.

"I remember thinking, 'Am I going to pack this thing up and have her treasure it? No.' When I moved out of that house, I left it."

The dollhouse episode explains why Melissa never lived with John in New York.

"I could never really put myself there," she said. "I just wanted to visit. In the old days there were some pretty shady characters roaming around, and things I didn't want any part of. There was some heavy-duty FBI in the barn, and some heavy-duty 'friends,' for lack of a better term.

But John never did any favors; he never did anything that would get him in trouble.

"I stayed three thousand miles away so I could raise my daughter correctly," she said, emphasizing: "There's never been any separation, just that I didn't want to be married to him, didn't want to live in New York, didn't want that lifestyle, didn't want to be around his craziness. I made the best of it. I had his daughter, and we figured it out. We were in touch all the time.

"John was always in the loop, and John was always paying for everything. He was in earnest, very conscientious, being three thousand miles away all the time, grabbing moments that he could with his daughter when we could travel there or she could travel there, and in the interim he was always trying to be there financially to make up for not being there physically."

John wasn't committed only to his daughter. Her brother felt it, too.

"To this day, what I remember is John always being there," Sam said. "Even though he wasn't always there in the flesh, he's always been there for my mom, always called my sister every day, always had a really strong presence in our lives. He wasn't necessarily an everyday father figure. But over the years he's always been somebody I could rely on or talk to. We've always had our own relationship, outside of my sister and outside of what my mom's relationship was with him. That's just the kind of guy he is.

"I value him, and I value what he's done for my mom; I value him as a dad to my sister. Even though he was who he was—you know, an interesting guy, a New Yorker, a Thoroughbred racehorse trainer, from an old-school Italian way of living—there's a code to that kind of gentleman, and he's definitely one of them."

Kentucky Calling

DAVID P. ROSELLE BEGAN HIS TERM as the ninth president of the University of Kentucky on July 1, 1987. Twelve days later, Rick Pitino was announced as the New York Knicks new head coach. Their paths intersected almost two years later, with a large assist from John Parisella.

The most successful program in college basketball by any of numerous measurements—most wins, highest winning percentage, most NCAA tournament bids, most tournament games and wins, and on—Kentucky had been the subject of a Pulitzer Prize-winning investigation into corruption in its storied basketball program by the *Lexington Herald-Leader* in 1985. And by 1987 UK was facing scrutiny by the National Collegiate Athletic Association (NCAA) for various academic and recruiting violations. Suspension of basketball competition for a year or two—the so-called NCAA Death Penalty—was a real possibility.

That didn't happen, many agree, largely because of President Roselle's swift and decisive actions. He quickly implemented institutional controls over the basketball program and moved the players' dorm, called Wildcat Lodge, from the athletic department to the university housing office. He replaced Kentucky legend Cliff Hagan as athletic director with C. M. Newton, whose reputation for integrity was without question. Roselle also forced coach Eddie Sutton to resign by making it clear he had lined up sufficient support to fire Sutton if he didn't quit.

And, with John Parisella working behind the scenes, he convinced Rick Pitino to come to Lexington and right the foundering ship.

I'm in California and I get a phone call from Shug McGaughey. He's trainer of the elite. The most famous and influential owner is the Phipps Stable, and he's the trainer.

Two boosters had called him and asked him if I could talk to Rick. "Can you go to your friend and see if he'd be interested in coaching Kentucky?" One of the boosters was Seth Hancock of Claiborne Farm.

Rick at the time was on his way out; Bianchi wanted to fire him. He was old school. And, really, most of the coaches in the NBA agreed that you couldn't press in the NBA the way Rick wanted to. That was college basketball.

Rick was going to have no place to go. I talked Bianchi into not firing him. I made him a promise that once Rick found another job, I would tell him before Rick told anybody else.

I told Rick about the call from McGaughey. The Knicks were going to make the playoffs; he said, "No. I'm not interested." Then things grew worse. He said he was interested.

The first time, I told McGaughey, "Tell your guys I'm sorry, he's still with the Knicks and he's got a shot at the playoffs." The second time I said, "Shug, he got back to me and he's definitely interested."

So Shug called the boosters, big money people—played gin rummy ten thousand a game, things like that. Boosters told him, "Okay, we're going to send C. M. Newton—A.D. at the time—to his house in Chappaqua. So Newton went and they had the interview. Newton left then Rick called me.

He said, "Why are you doing this, John? I have so much going on. They really don't want me."

> *I said, "Rick, that's why I don't like to get involved in these things. I have no control over it. You're getting mad at me again, and all I did was offer you something where they proposed to meet."*
>
> *He said, "Well, they're not interested. They don't want me."*

John had little choice but to go back to McGaughey, who was busy with a Triple Crown contender, Easy Goer (who won the Belmont that June).

> *I go to McGaughey and say, "Shug, listen. The A.D. goes there, and walks away. Rick said it was very nice, very cordial. But he left him with the feeling that you guys don't want him."*
>
> *So now the boosters turn to Shug and say, "Tell your friend John to ask Rick what he wants for us to get him there."*
>
> *So I call Rick and say, "Just listen to me, hear me out. What do you exactly want? Because they really want you. I don't care what your feelings are emotionally, or where your head is at; they really want you. This time I'm telling you. I really believe it, because they want to know what has to be done, and they'll tell you yes or no. Period."*
>
> *Rick says, "I want the president to fly into my home and tell me he wants me and he needs me."*

David Roselle had taught mathematics at the University of Maryland, Louisiana State University and Virginia Tech. He had served as secretary of the Mathematical Association of America for ten years. He had been provost at Virginia Tech, and was recognized nationally for pioneering campus computing and information systems. Two-and-a-half eventful years into his presidency at the University of Kentucky, Roselle would leave for the same job at the University of Delaware. He retired from that position seventeen years later.

> *I go back to McGaughey. I said, "Shug, if you feel this is going to be offensive to your people, don't do it. I mean it, because I think he's out of line. So it's your call."*
>
> *I told Rick what I was going to do. "What I'll do is I'll tell him what you want and I'll leave it up to him and them."*
>
> *Shug called up the boosters, and two days later the president went to his house and said, "We need you at Kentucky. We want you."*
>
> *That's how Rick got the job.*

Referring to the university's response to the allegations, NCAA Associate Executive Director Steve Morgan told a standing room-only press conference in Lexington: "I don't think I've ever seen a higher level of cooperation." Nonetheless, Kentucky's punishment included three years' probation, a two-year ban from postseason play, and a one-year loss of live television participation. On top of that, Pitino was taking over a team that had suffered Kentucky's first losing season (13-19) in sixty-one years.

> *It was all set up, but they had to go through the formalities of interviews. Rick was already the coach. I was standing there with Rick—I was there, naturally, because I was putting it together. I remember John Cheney (long-time Temple coach) walking out and saying to Rick, "These guys won't win three games."*
>
> *It might be the best coaching job of his career. He had no team. They had no talent. On the road he was one and twelve. At home he won thirteen and lost two—14-14 with these kids who couldn't play basketball! It was incredible!*

I saw every home game that year. Got thrown off the bench because I yelled at the referee on a bad call and Rick got a technical. He said, "John, I can't have you on the bench. I'll put you a couple rows behind the bench."

The next season Kentucky finished 22-6, and in 1991-92 returned to the NCAA Tournament, reaching the Elite Eight before losing to Duke 104-103 in overtime. In a tense game that stands as one of the most famous in the annals of March Madness, Duke's Christian Laettner caught a three-quarter-court inbounds pass in the final seconds and sank a shot from the foul line at the buzzer. A year later Kentucky reached the Final Four but lost to Michigan's Fab Five in the semifinals.

I say he's the best coach in college basketball, because he never had recruits like Duke or North Carolina. When he went to Kentucky, they were on suspension and had nothing.

* * *

AS PITINO FINISHED HIS FIRST SEASON at Kentucky, he was drawn into the state's gubernatorial campaign by Democrat Brereton Jones, who wanted the coach's endorsement. " ... it helps to understand how the passion surrounding basketball can influence other aspects of Kentucky life," Pitino wrote in *PITINO: My Story*. "By this ... I mean how passion for Kentucky basketball can affect state politics."

John, as usual, was the conduit. But he had to overcome the debilitating effects of losing the stable he'd built with Sabarese. He sent only twenty-five horses to the post in all of 1990 and forty-one in 1991, and told New York writers: "I was a wreck. After Sabarese I was afraid to fail. I was afraid to watch one of my horses come out of the gate, afraid of losing ... I was eating peanut butter and sleeping on a friend's couch." The intervention with Brereton Jones was just what John needed.

Brereton Jones is running for governor, and Pitino has the biggest pull in all of Kentucky. He came to me. I was acknowledged as Pitino's right-hand man, so anytime anybody in Kentucky wanted something from Pitino, they came to me. He thought he didn't know Pitino well enough to approach him.

I said, "I'll do this on one condition." He says, "Okay, name it, John." I said, "I want to spend one night with a broad in the Governor's Mansion." He says, "You got it."

The connection between John and Jones was, of course, horse racing. In 1972 Jones established Airdrie Stud on part of the old Woodburn Farm in Woodford County, ten miles from Lexington. Considered the birthplace of the Thoroughbred breeding industry, Woodburn Farm produced horses that won eighteen Triple Crown races in the late 1800s. But it became a cattle ranch in the early 1900s and remained so until Jones leased part of the land to establish the 2,500-acre Airdrie Stud.

With Pitino, and by extension Kentucky fans, behind him, Jones won the Democratic Primary in late May 1991, and defeated seven-term Republican Congressman Larry Hopkins by the largest margin in Kentucky history that November. Once in office he drew the ire of the General Assembly when he praised a federal investigation dubbed *Operation Boptrot*. (Boptrot stood for the Legislature's Business, Organization and Profession Committee, which oversaw state laws regulating horse racing in the state—the trot part of the acronym.)

I get a call at Ralph Willard's house—I don't know how he got the phone number. It's Brereton Jones. He says to me, "I'm going to need your help. I'm having problems with the wrong people. They're after me." I guess he knew about my family connections.

I said, "Okay," and hung up. Never did anything.

A month later I see him, and I say, "Is everything okay now?"

He says, "Aw, John, I can't thank you enough."

By 1995, when Jones' term as governor ended, seventeen people, including fifteen members of the Kentucky General Assembly, had been convicted or pled guilty to charges relating to *Operation Boptrot*. In 2004, Jones founded the Kentucky Equine Education Project, an organization dedicated to educating the public about Kentucky's horse industry and lobbying the General Assembly for more horse-friendly legislation. In October 2016, he received that organization's first Industry Vision Award for "significant contributions to Kentucky's horse industry."

Immediately after Jones left office (from the '95-'96 through '97-'98 seasons), Kentucky went to three straight Final Fours and won two national championships (a run exceeded only by John Wooden's seven straight national titles at UCLA from 1967 through 1973). Pitino was the Wildcats' head coach for the first two, and it was largely his team, playing for his successor, Tubby Smith, the third time.

In the 1996 semifinals, Kentucky beat Massachusetts and future UK coach John Calipari, before defeating Syracuse for the title. Putting the career of a star player ahead of his or his team's immediate interest the following season, Pitino lost the championship game to Arizona in overtime.

"I didn't play Derek Anderson (who had suffered a knee injury in January)," Pitino recalled. "I could have, because he was cleared medically; he practiced with us. But I just didn't feel comfortable with it. I felt he was going to be a lottery pick. He was coming off an injury. I didn't want to risk it.

"We play him, we win easily," Pitino said. "But I didn't play him. Miles Simon went off on us, and that's who Derek would have guarded."

The thirteenth player chosen in the NBA draft that June, Anderson played twelve seasons and scored more than seven thousand points as a pro.

"I have no regrets," Pitino said. "If he would have gotten hurt, I would never have forgiven myself."

Pitino returned to the NBA as coach of the Boston Celtics that summer, and—with seven of Pitino's players returning, Kentucky won it all again under Tubby Smith.

Gabbysaydada

SIMPLY REFERRING TO JOHN AS A proud father would be an understatement. It permeated his work as a trainer, right down to the names of some of his horses.

Gabby had not yet celebrated her first birthday (but had survived that hospital scare) when her dad named the first of two racehorses after her. Gabrielle P. went to the post for the first time on April 18, 1990, finishing sixth. She won a maiden claiming race July 1 that year, and was claimed two months later.

Then came Gabbysaydada, a name with obvious meaning. Foaled a month before Gabrielle P. entered the starting gate for the first time in an actual race, Gabbysaydada would compete sixty-one times in four years, though only seven of them for John before she, too, was claimed. Her first race occurred just after Gabby turned three, on September 20, 1992. She won for the first time the next month at Calder.

> *I was just so proud. I asked the owner if I could name a couple of horses after my daughter. He said, "Sure." I wanted a way to show what an important part of my life she was.*

Gabby was too young to know about Gabrielle P. or Gabbysaydada, but she had plenty of memories of being on the backside as a little girl. As she described it, she had no fear.

"You would find me in horses' stalls," she said. "I would see if the horses would lay down with me. Looking back, that was not smart. They're really crazy animals, especially Thoroughbreds—they have such a crazy temperament.

"In stalls," she continued, "there's, like, this thick plastic rope that keeps the horses in. I used to treat that like a monkey bar. I'd do flips and flips and flips and flips. I don't know how I got away without getting a foot to the head from a horse."

Gabby was in second grade when Roxy the miniature horse entered her life.

"I remember going to get her and it being farm-like," she said. "Whenever I went to visit, I almost looked more forward to visiting her than seeing anyone else, other than my dad. I grew up giving her donuts from Dunkin' Donuts as a kid, then as an adult I would feed her my coffee. So we came full circle."

Riding in Angel Cordero's cart with his kids is what led Gabby to Roxy.

"They had the wagon; that's why I wanted a miniature horse for myself. I remember their pony so well. He was chestnut color—not as cute as Roxy. Roxy was white and black with big spots, like a painted miniature pony, with the big black forelocks that looked like an Afro on her forehead."

Seeing her dad only when he visited her in California or she visited him, usually in New York, was not as big a deal for Gabby as some might expect. Nor was not having him around her home regularly.

"Whenever anyone asks me about my dad being so far away," she said, "I just don't know any different. I had such a good childhood that I never think, like, 'Oh, my dad wasn't there.' My unconventional pieces just fit together. I had a lot better childhood than a lot of people did with their parents both in the house. It's just what I know. I would see him a few times throughout the year, but definitely every summer and Christmas. We have so many fun memories."

John Nash helped make some of those memories when he was with the Philadelphia 76ers, through his brother Tom. "He was in the ticket business," Nash said. "He worked for a company called Electric Factory Concerts that promoted all the major concerts in Philadelphia.

So whenever John and his daughter needed tickets, he was able to fix them up."

Nash met John the year Gabby was born. "He was in the press room at The Spectrum with Rick Pitino," he recalled. "They were very close, and John would come to Philadelphia when the Knicks played the Sixers.

"I knew who he was, but we never had a relationship. Then in 1996 we had a mutual friend, Ed Stefanski, who knew John from Atlantic City Race Track."

Like Nash, Ed Stefanski enjoyed a long career as a pro basketball executive. Between 2004 and 2017 he was in charge of basketball operations for the New Jersey Nets, Philadelphia 76ers, Toronto Raptors and Memphis Grizzlies. In 2018 he was named senior advisor to the owner of the Detroit Pistons, in charge of reorganizing the front office and coaching staff. Under his leadership, Detroit made the NBA playoffs in 2019 for only the second time in ten seasons.

"Eddie called me—he knew I had an interest in horses, as he did— and he said, 'My friend John Parisella is going to be at Delaware Park. We ought to get a horse together.' So we went and met John for dinner. We claimed a horse. And from that point, I was pretty frequently around the barn. Over the years he trained several horses for us."

Gabby, of course, knew none of this as she enjoyed concerts most girls could only dream of attending.

"At the time, because I was a kid, I didn't really understand why my dad had the connections that he did," Gabby said. "He lived in New York, but every time we went out there we would take a limo to Philly because he had a connection with the Sixers. We saw Backstreet Boys ... *Nsync ... Usher ... Spice Girls. So a lot of my fondest memories as a kid were in Philadelphia because his connections were there.

"And then every Christmas we'd see a Broadway show, and he knew someone from the track who was working backstage, and I'd be able to go backstage for every single Broadway show we went to. I remember the first time I realized that it was his connections that did it. I really wanted to see *Elf,* the Christmas movie that turned Broadway. He didn't know anyone working it, and he didn't know how to get tickets. So we had to figure that out. He felt really badly that it wasn't "special" in his words. I said, 'Dad, no. I'm just happy to go to the show. I'm in New York and it's Christmastime, and I'm going to a Broadway show.'"

Gabby experienced John's "down" side, too, at least once, though it was just a fun adventure at her age. It's reminiscent of the time Pasquale took young John to the track in Jamaica, New York in the Italian tradition, for luck.

> *It was one of the low points in my career. I really had nothing going for me, so I had to figure out a way to generate money. I had a credit balance from my contract with Sabarese. He was a big craps player. So I was able to get a $10,000 credit line. I had to find a way to get to Vegas, so I borrowed money from three friends. Plane fare.*
>
> *What I did was go to California. My daughter was six, maybe seven. I picked her up and took her to Vegas for luck. I thought I was going to play the games, but what I did was go to the Sports Room.*
>
> *Kentucky was playing Tennessee. On paper I just couldn't see them losing. Now did I get Pitino's opinion on the game? No. He views it that every game is going to be tough ... There's no easy game. That's why he's a winner. So I didn't want any part of his opinion. I was giving points. This was me.*
>
> *I bet the ten thousand on the game at Caesar's Palace, and I took a room. I sat with my daughter on the edge of the bed, and we watched the game together. The team won very easily. Wow! Won nine thousand—because of the vig (the bookmaker's cut for taking the risk of the bet, called vigorish).*

So I'm having a couple tequilas and playing the slot machines, running around with my daughter. And the security guards are chasing us—during which time her mother called police; they're looking for me. We hopped on a plane and went back to California.

It was mission accomplished: I love my daughter; I spent time with her. I was out of a big hole. Paid my friends back the airfare; paid back the six thousand I was in the hole for; and wound up with a couple thousand in my pocket.

Gabby became a standout soccer player at San Ramon Valley High School, on the Mustang Soccer Club's elite Mustang Fury team, and ultimately as a Division One scholarship player at Loyola Marymount University—"top dog, queen of the field, captain (if we had one) and the downright leader," wrote Courtney Jones, a member of the wedding party, on the Gabrielle Parisella-Robbie Vaughan Wedding website in the spring of 2018. In her comments on the site, Courtney described Gabby in ways that sounded very much like she was describing John: "... loyal to no limit ... the biggest heart you can find."

Soccer dominated Gabby's youth the way baseball, football or basketball consumed a young boy's growing-up years for much of the 20th Century.

"Since I was eight years old we traveled ten times a year all over the country," she said. "We were ranked Number One in the country numerous times; I don't remember what years. Everyone on our team, even the ones on our bench, all went and played Division One (collegiate) soccer."

I saw her play twice. When it comes to my daughter, I get so nervous and caught up inside. I'm just focusing on her doing well. Nothing matters but her.

Soccer trips sometimes took Gabby as far as New York, which enabled her to spend time with John, usually at Saratoga, joined by another of her eventual bridesmaids—"my best friend, Hannah. Her dad's from New York, as well, and her parents related to our dynamic and would let her come with me a lot. I remember running around Saratoga with her."

"Between all the trips to New York in the summers to visit Gabby's dad, and traveling all over the country for soccer, we were inseparable ..." Hannah Marsala wrote on Gabby's wedding website. "Our interests include *Nsync, New York pizza, ESPN, magic markers and horse races."

Injuries and surgeries (knee, ankle, foot), concussions and adulthood ended Gabby's playing career. ("Playing professionally was never a question because I wanted a career after college.") She became an elementary school teacher and a Mustang coach. ("I coach with the same coaches who coached me.") She and Robbie settled in San Jose after their wedding, requiring a 45-minute commute to her fifth-grade class at Tassajara Hills Elementary in Danville. ("I call my dad every day on my ride home," she said; usually they talked sports, John's favorite TV shows and what was going on in their lives that day.)

"It all started when I was in sixth grade, when cell phones came out," she recalled. "I got one and he'd actually call me every morning and be my alarm clock when I was a kid. We probably talk more than we text because, as a teacher, it's hard to have text conversations. But he sends me a text every day."

> *I express my love ... make sure she knows how much I miss her ... tell her she's the most important thing in my life. Three thousand miles away, I wanted to make sure she knew. Her mother didn't want her to have a cell phone in the sixth grade, but it was how I could stay connected with her.*

Homestretch

1996 Turfway Park-Winter/Spring Meet
Leading Trainer--John Parisella
New Record-40 Wins in a Single Meet

Previous page: Rick Pitino and John Parisella in 1996 *(photo courtesy of Melissa Sanders);* and John after setting the Turfway Park single meet record for wins by a trainer *(Pat Lang Photography, courtesy of Turfway Park)*

Glory Year

THE YEAR OF RICK PITINO'S ULTIMATE success at the University of Kentucky, 1996, was a glory year for John Parisella, too. Partners in irony, Pitino was completing the resurrection of a basketball program in shambles only a few years before, while John was rebuilding his racing stable after a more immediate crisis. Things had begun uncertainly for the coach's friend because of another disagreement with Ken Noe, whose decision to cut John's stall space at Aqueduct preceded the off-site barn fire that claimed eighteen of John's horses in 1972. By 1995 Noe had become NYRA president, and he barred John from New York racetracks after a shouting match between them.

"Ken was a real tough guy," said John's friend Ken Dunn, who was Noe's close friend, too. "If he was your friend, you couldn't have a better friend. If he was your enemy, you couldn't have a worse enemy. He didn't like people who didn't play by the rules."

> *When he was boosted up to be in charge of everything, he couldn't wait to throw me off the grounds. He was super ultraconservative, very caring about the business. I was on the wild side, and that's the complete opposite, the antithesis of what he was. Plus we had that argument, and I did so much yelling that he barred me from the track. He just didn't want me there.*
>
> *It turned out to be a blessing for me.*

With only a handful of horses and no support team to accompany him, John wound up at Turfway Park in Northern Kentucky, about seventy miles up Interstate 75 from Lexington, for its 1995-96 Winter/Spring Meet. D. Wayne Lukas was there, too, the acknowledged "name" trainer on the backside. Four months later, John had set the track record for most wins by a trainer in one racing meeting.

> *He (Lukas) paid me a great compliment when I broke the record at Turfway. He told everyone: "When it comes to winter, you'll never beat John Parisella."*
>
> *What made me choose Kentucky? I honestly don't know. Maybe it was because Rick was coaching there. That could have been the only reason, actually. Morris Bailey, who played an important role in my life as well as Rick, thought it wouldn't be the right place to go. Most of the times they were right in my life. I also agreed with them, believe it or not, but I still went ahead and did it.*
>
> *Wayne Lukas had forty horses, and six or seven other known trainers had twenty-five to thirty each. I wish I could have made a bet on me in Las Vegas, because my odds had to be 100-to-1. I had nothing. Zero. Broke.*
>
> *I went there with eight horses, and my best horse got hurt as soon as I got there, Danzig's Dance. I was totally counting on him. So now I'm totally lost. Then another got hurt. I was down to six.*
>
> *I needed a few more horses, so I called Morris Bailey. I said, "Morris, I want to borrow fifty thousand." He says, "Why?"*
>
> *I said, "I'll pay you back in four months." He said, "You're going to pay me back in four months. How are you going to do that?"*

I said, "What business is it of yours? Did I ask you how you were going to pay me back when I loaned you money?"

So he sent the fifty thousand. With that, I got a couple extra horses.

Besides enough horses, John needed a support team. He was starting from scratch in unfamiliar surroundings.

In many other states I could have put a team together right away. But I had no experience there, so it was very difficult finding a jockey, exercise rider, blacksmith. I couldn't afford to bring a team with me.

I had so few horses, I had to tell the best blacksmith and exercise rider: "Please, I'll work with whatever time you want; fit me in." If I don't put a team together, I don't win, let alone break the record.

John faced another obstacle of his own making, one that reflected Ted Sabarese's view of the way John had been received at the Kentucky Derby years earlier. Sabarese had said: "In those circles you're rubbing shoulders with people who don't go for Brooklyn kind of people." Never one to hold back or choose his words diplomatically, John had been quoted in a 1994 *Daily Racing Form* story saying:

"I'm tired of these bigots in Kentucky who believe that you have to wear a green jacket, khakis and penny loafers in order to be considered a trainer. They have a real prejudice against certain people—especially Italians and Jews from New York—and it doesn't matter what these people do, they aren't going to get the good Kentucky horses.

"I was talking with a major Kentucky owner, who had seen what I was doing in New York and was considering sending me some horses. It turns out that some bigoted Kentucky breeder stuck his nose in my business, told the owner that I was crazy and didn't fit in. It cost me that owner.

"Doesn't it make you wonder why people like Pete Ferriola, Gasper Moschera, Bruce Levine, Frank LaBoccetta, Butch Lenzini and Dick Dutrow can do amazing things with horses and never are given a chance to train good horses? They develop horses they claim, and they have great results, yet none of these Kentucky bigots will give them a shot.

"I've seen this for a long time, but having it happen to me finally made me speak out."

Copyrighted c. 2019 by Daily Racing Form, LLC.
Reprinted with Permission of the Copyright owner.

After the story appeared and was picked up in the Lexington newspaper, Pitino tried to counsel John.

They went nuts in Kentucky because it implied bias. They knew about my relationship with Rick, so they all went running to him. He calls me and says, "You know anything about this?" He said, "John, you gotta find a way to put in a retraction." In fact, I wanted to say more.

As soon as I got to Turfway, the track steward called me in and said, "Hotshots from New York not only aren't going to get special treatment, but we're going to be looking very closely." That wasn't very welcoming to me. But I was at a point in my life where I was thrown out of New York so it didn't really mean anything to me.

They considered me an outsider. It was a lot to overcome.

Kentucky had fallen one game short of the Final Four in 1995, losing by thirteen to North Carolina in the Southeast Regional championship game. With nine future NBA players on the roster, Pitino's Wildcats were ranked No. 1 as the '95-'96 season began. They lost the second game of the season—to Calipari's Massachusetts team that featured eventual College Player of the Year Marcus Camby—then won twenty-five in a row to finish the regular season 26-1. They lost again to Mississippi State in the Southeastern Conference Tournament, to go into March Madness 28-2.

As that season unfolded, John and Pitino made regular trips to each other's venue.

I had to win over the people who were working in the office at the track. I was able to establish that because they were all wonderful people.

What helped me with the people at Turfway is that Rick would come up and root for me. It gave me a lot of exposure to have Rick coming there.

We were driving an hour either way, me to practice, him to see me race. I'd fall asleep in the stands, and he'd throw the ball into the stands at me. I saw every home game, all fourteen.

There was time for fun, too, when John visited Kentucky practices and when they had time to socialize.

His son was 15 or 16 at the time. He played some basketball. They loved to tease me. He said, "Oh, I could beat you. It would be no contest."

Right away, Rick says, "I heard that. I'll bet you $20 you can't beat him. You can't beat Horse." He's betting on me against his son! His son says okay.

> *The score is tied near the finish. And then I hear Rick yelling from the stands, "I told you, he can't go to his left. He can only go to his right. If you listen to me, you have to win this game."*
>
> *Sure enough, I played it so he had to go to his left, and I won the game. His son walked out pissed. He didn't pay his father.*

And then there was the night John and Ken Dunn and his wife went to dinner in Lexington with Pitino and his wife Joanne.

"Rick had a restaurant called Pitino Bravo," Dunn recalled. "We run into ex-Miss America, Gov. Brown's ex-wife, Phyllis George. She wants Rick to come to her house for dinner.

"When we go to her house for dinner, she has a couple of friends there, and one of them is Kenny Rogers' ex-wife, Marianne Gordon, who is a gorgeous blonde. All night through dinner, John is trying to hustle her—and not very successfully. So we're all gathered by the door, ready to walk out, saying our thank-yous and goodbyes, and just as we're starting to go out the door, John turns to her and says: 'Listen, before I go, I've gotta ask you a question. Did you ever learn when to hold 'em and when to fold 'em?'

"She got crimson red and not very happy. I guess he figured, 'I wasn't able to convince her to go out, so I'll take a little shot at the end.'"

John acknowledges Dunn's sequence of events but challenges his conclusion.

> *She got a big kick out of it, and that really opened the door. After that I figured I might as well ask her out. And she was willing. But she lived in Atlanta. I never went out with her because she lived there.*

* * *

TURFWAY PARK'S MEDIA GUIDE DOCUMENTED John's unprecedented success in 1996, noting that his forty first-place finishers beat by nine the old record, set by Tom Dorris fifteen years earlier, and that he won 33% of his starts. (On March 16 that year John set a personal record by winning four straight races.) An accompanying table showed D. Wayne Lukas second with thirty-seven firsts, a still very good 21%. John won No. 40 on the last day with jockey Robbie Davis, and that's a story in itself.

It was Davis whose mount went down at Belmont in 1988 and crushed the skull of Mike Venezia, in whose honor the award recognizing "extraordinary sportsmanship and citizenship" was created. After the accident, Davis had gone into seclusion in Idaho with his wife and three children, wracked by severe depression. He returned to racing five months later, and in 1997 received the Mike Venezia Memorial Award.

I spent time with Robbie. Being strongly religious myself, I could relate to him. We formed a very close relationship by me trying to help him.

As fate would have it, he came in twice to ride at Turfway. We were so happy to see each other.

First time, I went to the agent and said, "Please understand. He's only coming in once, and he's like family to me. So I want to put him on this particular horse." And the horse won.

Then he showed up a second time, on the last day, and I did the same thing. I put him on a horse. And winning that race for me with a great ride, I set the record (which stood for more than twenty years).

Pitino took time to call John from the first round of the NCAA basketball tournament in Dallas, where Kentucky advanced by beating San Jose State and Virginia Tech, to congratulate him the day John won those four straight races. But he couldn't see the record-setting race—for good reason. He was at The Meadowlands Sports Complex in New Jersey for the Final Four. As Kentucky avenged its early season loss to UMass in the semifinals, John ran one of the coach's horses, Mr. Tyler, in the Hansel Stakes. He hoped for a victory as a present and good omen for his close friend, but Mr. Tyler finished third. The next day John won his fortieth race at Turfway, and the day after that, Kentucky beat Syracuse 76-67 for Pitino's first national championship. John was there to see it.

He compared his record after starting with only eight horses to Pitino's first season at Kentucky, when he coached a team with no player taller than six-foot-seven to that improbable 14-14 record. "When I came here," John told a reporter, "I kept in mind his work ethic in that situation. I marveled at what he did."

Following their twin achievements, the matter of John's ban from New York racing remained to be resolved. This time it was Pitino who did the fixing.

> *I spent some time with Rick when he came up to Saratoga that summer. He loves Saratoga and spent a couple weeks up there.*
>
> *Rick says, "John, you have to get back to training in New York." I said, "I can't." I told him how Noe even barred me from the paddock.*
>
> *He says, "There's gotta be a way. You've got to go and apologize—keep apologizing until you get back there. This is your home. You're great at what you do. The whole world knows you. You've got to make sure it happens."*
>
> *So now we're sitting in his house. He's on the couch and I'm in a chair, and he says to me: "I'll tell you what. Here's what I'll do for you. Two conditions. I will write the letter of apology, but you have to sign it and you have to deliver it. But I will write the letter."*

I told him, "I'm not reading it." He says, "You don't have to. Just sign it and deliver it."

He wrote the letter and I never read it. To this day I never read it. Ken Noe had no idea it was coming from Pitino.

So Rick wrote the letter. I signed it—never read it. And very uncomfortably, I made sure he wasn't in the office and left it with his secretary, Florence. I didn't want to apologize; I didn't want any part of even running into him.

Couple hours later, Rick's in the box, and Ken comes running over to him because he knew how much Rick wanted me back. He says, "Your friend did the right thing. See what he did. Look at the letter he wrote me. Now he's coming back. It's no problem. Everything's okay. Everything's good."

"I just told it like he wanted to give this letter, wanted to apologize for whatever he did," Pitino said. "I write a lot better than John; I acted more humble; and he got back in his good graces. John knew it was the right thing to do."

John's relationship with Ken Noe ended on a positive note before Noe died in 2013.

He would come to Saratoga, and at the end of his life he says, "John, you were always a great horseman. I'm proud of you."

The Racing Game

WHAT JOHN CALLED THE RACING GAME is a colorful, diverse world, one in which he alternately thrived and crashed for almost fifty years. At one end of the spectrum are the breeders and their lush horse farms; owners who range from very wealthy to "comfortable enough" that they could throw in with others to buy a horse or maybe a handful; and the trainers, some of whom make a good living (or better) and others who scrape by. At different times, John fell into both categories.

Those jockeys who ride the top horses in the big races—Angel Cordero Jr., for example—are well-known and financially successful. But most are closer to the other end of the spectrum where grooms, exercise riders, hot-walkers and other barn regulars live paycheck to paycheck or often fall short and need a hand.

In the stands and at the rail are the horseplayers—from those who pore over the charts in *The Daily Racing Form* to those who keep their own past performance records, and the casual bettors who might choose which horse to back simply by name or the color of a stable's silks.

The trainers, in particular, form relationships that reflect all aspects and realities of the backside community. John became close to many fellow trainers over five decades, and none reflect the personal and lasting nature of life in and around the barns better than his friendships with Gary Gullo, Bruce Levine, Scott Lake and Anthony Margotta Jr.

Levine got to know John when he was just starting at the bottom, in much the way John had. "I was rubbing horses for John Campo," he said. "John (Parisella) had stalls at the other end of the barn. He was very friendly. He was one of the two trainers who signed for my trainer's license; you had to have two."

> *He was one of my best friends on the track. In the morning there are all these trainers down by the rail, and he and I spent most of our time talking together, about horses, our problems, whatever it might be.*
>
> *Everybody loves to win in this game. I loved to win much more than him; I was obsessed, whereas he wasn't. What's great about him is, he was low-key. I was always flying high, and he was low-key. He offered me balance, which is very important.*

Levine described the horse-trainer profession this way:

"In this game you gotta put it away for a rainy day. You could equate it to a couple of these heavyweight champion boxers. They're winning all this money then they get the women, the booze, the drugs, the hanger-oners. All of a sudden, a guy loses a fight and it breaks up.

"You see guys in the Hall of Fame, and they've got no horses. It's a very tough, tough business—a lot more downs than ups in this game. You really gotta plan for the rainy day, because when it stops, it stops sudden and hard. In 2008-2009, I'm training a hundred horses; now (ten years later) I got thirty horses.

"It'll stop on you in a dime. It just stops. This horse gets hurt; that horse gets hurt; and the next thing you know you get fired or your owner goes belly-up. This owner takes horses away from you, and you're almost unemployed. It's a very difficult game."

Off-Track-Betting, or OTB, which enabled horseplayers to bet on races without going to the track, was approved in New York in 1970. Simulcasting races—real-time video showings of one track's races at another betting location—began in 1983 and was approved by voters in

1985 after the New Jersey Supreme Court suspended the practice. Those two developments changed The Racing Game forever. Bruce Levine explained:

"An hour before first post they'd lock all the phones up. You couldn't make a phone call at the racetrack because they were afraid you were calling a bookmaker. You couldn't make a phone call. If you wanted to call someone you basically had to get a stamp on your hand and go down the block—almost like in the movie "The Sting." With simulcasts, people want to bet on better horses at bigger tracks. So today you have fewer horses, fewer tracks."

As a result of the simulcasts, attendance at the track is so low that it has taken the life out of the game, which is the excitement of the crowd.

Also there isn't the camaraderie after the races, with guys hanging out at the track. Agents and trainers rely on the phones instead of live interaction to communicate.

* * *

BORN IN 1965, THE SAME YEAR John began working for John Campo, Scott Lake won his first race in 1984, the year after John started training for Ted Sabarese. In 2010 Lake became the sixth-leading trainer in North America for career victories, and by 2018 had a shot at reaching fourth on the all-time list if he stayed in the game to normal retirement age. (Through 2018, his win total stood at 5,960—21.3%, and his in-the-money finishers numbered 14,749—52.8%.)

Lake and John met in the late Nineties.

"When I was a kid, growing up and watching racing, John was a big name," he said. "To actually meet him was, like, 'Wow! I'm meeting John Parisella.' I was just a small guy then, trying to get out of Penn National and move forward. John helped me when I moved to New York;

put me in touch with some of the right people, told me who to deal with and who to stay away from as far as owners went—stuff like that. He showed me the ropes."

> *He's somebody I liked to be around because, for a guy who did so much winning, he was very humble. In this game, you have a tendency to not be.*

Lake experienced the kind of ups and downs Levine described and John endured, and exhibited John's kind of charity in the face of it. Victimized by a person he trusted to handle his finances while he focused on training horses and winning races, Lake found himself owing $2 million in back taxes as well as swindled out of another $2 million. But rather than pursue prosecution or retribution, he chose to focus on rebuilding his own life.

It wasn't easy, but Lake survived. "He's that kind of guy," John said.

"The first and second nights, I couldn't sleep," Lake said. "The third night, I remember I got up in the middle of the night to go to the bathroom, and I'm standing there, thinking to myself: 'You know what? I've got two little kids in the next room that absolutely love me. I've got a daughter in Harrisburg who absolutely loves me. Who cares!' From that time on, I slept like a baby and never let it stress me again.

"It wasn't like it put me out of business. At that time I had two hundred eighty horses in training. It caused me to scale back, and keep scaling back."

Years after John saddled his last racehorse, Lake and John remained close friends. "John and I, we can not talk for four or five months," he said, "and when we pick up the phone it's like we were hanging out last night."

Lake, in fact, was among the guests attending the wedding of John's daughter, Gabby. "He didn't invite a whole lot of racetrack people," he said. "I was completely honored that he invited me and my girlfriend, that he thought that much of our friendship."

As much as John meant to him, though, and as much as Lake overcame, the Anthony Margotta Jr. story may top it.

FEAR NOT
I have redeemed you.
I have called you by name.
You are mine.

—Isaiah 43:1

Lifesaver

THE EARLY MORNING TEXT MESSAGES with passages from Scripture began arriving sometime in 2015. It was Anthony Margotta Jr.'s way of giving back to the man he says saved his life.

"John Parisella and his encouragement and his life story had a large part to do with my recovery from alcohol and drugs," Margotta said, "because he had struggled early on in his career as a horse trainer with substance abuse like I did. During my most trying times, he was there. And really ... I can't tell you ... God does work in mysterious ways. He put John in my life at the time when I really needed somebody to help me get through it."

Twenty years younger than John, Margotta wasn't yet a teenager when the "Trainer to the Stars" was careening up and down the California coast and across New York, his life in disarray. It would be another twenty years before their paths crossed.

"I came into this because my father and uncle were gamblers and bookmakers," Margotta said, the similarity to John Parisella's youth apparent though not to Anthony. "I used to go to the track with them.

When I was getting ready to graduate from high school, they said, 'Whaddya going to do? Whaddya want to do with your life?'

"These guys used to go out and gamble all day, then go to casinos at night; go out to dinner, wear suits and drive Cadillacs. I said, 'Whaddya mean, what am I going to do? I'm going to do what you guys do. What's better than this?'

"With the finger, you know, the wave of the finger, they're like, 'No, no, no. You're not going to do what we do.' My uncle had done time in jail. He was a real, live gangster. He was one of John Gotti's henchmen: Robert Bisaccia. He did life and died in prison.

"They said, 'Why don't you go over and learn how to train horses?' The closest I'd ever been to a horse was leaning over the rail, looking at him coming out on the track to bet on him. I said, 'I'd like to do that, but I don't know.'"

Anthony's uncle told him to meet him "down at the club on Tuesday," so Anthony went to the neighborhood social club as told, and wound up working for J.J. Crupi, a fixture in New Jersey racing for thirty years who won the leading trainer title at Monmouth Park four times and at The Meadowlands once. Crupi later founded New Castle Farm, a full-service horse farm in Ocala, Florida. The 2017 Kentucky Derby winner, Always Dreaming, did his early training at New Castle, and two entries in the 2018 Derby—Audible and Vino Rosso—trained there, too.

"I was 18 when I started as a hot-walker," Margotta said. "John Parisella was already a well-known horse trainer who had won a lot of big races. So first, I just knew him by name alone. First time I saw him was at Hialeah. When you're a young guy, you see someone like that and you're starstruck.

"As the years went by, I became a trainer and met John on the level of working in the same industry and competing with him. I always admired John. John was a very successful horse trainer, always won big races, trained for big clients, well-known people. I strived to be a top trainer myself, so he was one I liked to emulate."

Anthony Margotta Jr. didn't have drug addiction in mind when he envisioned emulating John, but he emulated him in that way, too. He evolved into one of the early casualties of the opioid crisis that became one of the political themes of the 2016 presidential campaign and the years that followed.

"As horse trainers, we move a lot of hay, move water buckets'" he said. "I started with one horse; I was hands-on. Around 1988-1990 I went to a doctor and told him, 'I have a lot of back pain.' He prescribed me painkillers—Vicodin and Percocet. I started taking them. Who knew they would be addictive?"

Percocet is a brand name for the combination of the pain reliever acetaminophen and the narcotic oxycodone, and is used to treat "moderate to severe" pain, according to WebMD. It is a controlled substance with a "high risk for addiction and dependence," according to drugfree.org. Vicodin, a combination of acetaminophen and the opioid hydrocodone, has similar risks.

"By '95-'96," Margotta continued, "I'm now doctor-shopping and getting ninety to a hundred pills from three different doctors. When you're taking fifteen Percocets a day, that adds up.

"Toward the late Nineties it became a problem. I was dependent on the opioid prescription pain pills. It really started taking a toll on me physically, mentally. It was a very bad time. I knew I was in some serious trouble. I was addicted and I couldn't get as many as I needed. So I started drinking, also, to ease the pain when I didn't have them."

Margotta was living with a jockey's agent named Barry Brown in a house in Atlantic City when Brown offered John a place to stay. It proved to be the turning point in Anthony's life, though salvation didn't happen overnight.

> *I remember it vividly. He was wasting away on drugs. His business was shot. He was on that road to self-destruction and*

you could see each day he got a little closer, not knowing when it was going to happen but each day getting a little worse.

"We spent a lot of time together," Margotta said. "He really was like a big brother to me during a very dark time in my life. He explained that he had had a substance-abuse problem with cocaine and it cost him dearly. He said, 'Tony, listen, I went through what you're going through now, and here I am today. I got through it, so I know you can.' I had no idea he had those demons. I didn't know his personal struggles. Once he started sharing his personal struggles with me, we instantaneously became like brothers; we bonded.

"There's an article about him when he hit bottom, sleeping at friends' houses and stuff like that. He had it laminated and had it in his office at Saratoga. They're not very good stories to share; not many people will come out and share that stuff. What it did for me as I was going through that, I was listening to John tell me that what I was going through, he'd been there."

By then, John had saddled a pair of Kentucky Derby contenders and had trained the heralded Simply Majestic.

"Here's a guy I wanted to be like," Margotta said, "and to hear him say, 'There's nothing wrong with you. You just have a disease and we need to get you some help.' It saved my life. It was John Parisella who was there at a crucial time in my life, who was kind enough not to judge me but to be a guy who knows.

"It's like the old story: A guy falls down a manhole and says, 'How do I get out of here?' A priest walks by and says, 'I'll pray for you.' A social worker comes by and says, 'Come by my office this afternoon and I'll get you out of there.' Then a doctor comes by and says, 'I'll prescribe something and get you out of there.' Then John comes along, sees me in the manhole, and jumps down in the manhole and says, 'Follow me. I'll get you out of here.'"

Margotta dropped out of racing for close to a decade and lost virtually everything—his wife, homes in Saratoga Springs and South Florida, interest in a Boca Raton restaurant—before he turned his life around. "Unfortunately, I didn't get it right away," he admitted.

Anthony had introduced Saul Kupferberg and his dad Max to horse racing, and had been their only trainer for more than a decade. A member of the first class at Queens College, where he majored in physics, Max worked on the Manhattan Project, which developed the atomic bomb during World War II, then co-founded the Flushing, N.Y.-based electronic equipment manufacturing company Kepco Inc. Saul, who eventually worked in his dad's company, had bought into a racing partnership while living in Philadelphia, and a short time later his father said, "Why don't we buy some racehorses together?"

In 2000, when Anthony made the decision to leave racing until he got his life back together, he played matchmaker between the Kupferbergs and John.

"The Kupferbergs were the most loyal people in the world," Anthony said. "I wanted to make sure they were in good hands. I suggested that they interview John Parisella. I knew John was a very good horse trainer. I knew he was the right guy to turn their horses over to. They met and clicked right away. John trained for them for quite a few years."

At first, though, John declined the opportunity—for reasons that define him.

It's the way I'm made. I'd never take a horse away from a friend. I love Anthony, so I'm not going to take his horses. They can find somebody else.

That night, Anthony called me. We sat down, and he said, "John, what's the matter with you? You're only hurting yourself. And in a way, it takes away from me saying you deserve this. It's not doing me any good if you refuse them."

> *I knew Anthony sent them to me, but I wasn't going to buy into it. I'm very strong on that. It's one of my close friends. I'm not going to take the horses and do well and have them not go back to him. I'm not into that.*
>
> *He said, "You're an idiot. It's not going to do me any good if you don't take the horses. You showed your allegiance. Let's call them right now and tell them you'll take them."*

That's what they did, and John enjoyed almost immediate success after taking over the Kupferberg stable at Saratoga in 2000. Then, between April 20 and the end of May in 2001, he won eight of nine starts at Aqueduct and Belmont and lost by a neck in the other race. The hot hand led others to ask if he would train their horses, too, but he declined all overtures. "I don't want anybody else right now," he said at the time, echoing his friend Anthony's sentiments. "These people have been great. I want to enjoy the year with them."

There was one exception in 2001, though, when John honored a promise he'd made to New York City radio sports talk icon Mike Francesa a decade earlier. The "Mike" in WFAN's popular "Mike and the Mad Dog" drive-time show (with Chris Russo) from 1989 to 2008, Francesa later became the solo leader in Big Apple sports talk. Before he began his radio career, *The New Yorker* once referred to Francesa as Brent Musberger's brain, a nod to his behind-the-scenes work as a researcher and analyst for CBS Sports in the early 1980s.

> *My favorite show was listening to Mike on The Fan. He was the most knowledgeable of all the people I listened to. Our paths crossed at Aqueduct and Belmont.*
>
> *I wanted to be friendly with him because I had so many sports questions for him. And him being a good guy, he always spent the time to answer them.*

> *Rick Pitino asked me one day if I knew Mike. I said, "All I can tell you is he's a good guy. You know me; I'll go up and ask any questions about sports. And he is nice enough to listen to me."*

Pitino was still head coach of the New York Knicks. He'd soon leave pro basketball for the University of Kentucky, but neither he nor John knew that at the time.

> *Rick asked me: "He really doesn't know that much about me, John, so will you spend time talking to him about me?" I told Rick, "Sure."*

> *I ran into Mike in the Trustees Room at Belmont Park and said, "Mike, do you have a few minutes?" He said, "Sure, John. What is it?"*

> *I said to him, "Let me tell you a few things about Rick Pitino and what he's all about." And he listened.*

> *Finally, he says, "Okay, I understand where you're coming from, and I'll do this under one condition: that you train a horse for me." I said, "Okay, you got a deal."*

Francesa was not yet an owner, so John didn't hold up his end of the bargain immediately. A decade later, after Francesa acquired some Thoroughbreds, John trained a mare named *Emociones* during 2001 and 2002, and won one of seven races with her.

> *Mike was one of my favorite owners because I was a sports fanatic and he loved horse racing and was so knowledgeable about sports.*

As John's friendship with Francesa developed, he had some fun at Saratoga with Hall of Fame football coach Bill Parcels, who won two Super Bowls with the New York Giants.

Mike and I meet up at Saratoga, and one day we sit in the box with Bill Parcels, who is one of Mike's best friends. After we sat in the box for several hours, Parcels—being on the quiet side, and me, I'm rambunctious—turned to me and said, "You know, you would like my brother better." And we all started laughing.

Bill and I, when Mike wasn't there, sat in the box and made dollar bets on which horse would finish last in each race. I had a lot of fun with him.

Still training for Saul and Max Kupferberg, John produced thirty winners in 2013—making them No. 100 among owners nationally that year. He was in the news then, too, for his trademark ability to turn claimers into winners.

"Since John Parisella claimed Sunny Desert for $35,000, the filly has gone from a sulking maiden to a four-time stakes winner," began one story. "So what does the trainer credit for the turnaround?"

John had an unusual, but for him typical, explanation for Sunny Desert's six-race winning streak.

She was a maiden filly, and she would always stay in the back of the stall, which is a sign that a horse is not happy and something is bothering them.

I tried everything, like carrots . . . apples . . . greens, and nothing worked. So out of desperation, I fed her peppermints. And all of a sudden she starts winning, including stakes races.

The familiarity between her and me became incredible after that. I have the tendency to be loud. And when I would be walking on the track to watch her train and she'd hear my voice, she would whinny as if to say "hello."

You can't imagine what that made me feel like inside.

* * *

FOR MOST OF THE FIRST DECADE of the new millennium, Anthony Margotta was, by his description, spiraling out of control. "Some sobriety, then fall back," he said. "I wound up homeless on the streets of north New Jersey, where I was born." Eventually, he turned to Alcoholics Anonymous, which helped him stay sober and off drugs. Through it all, the one constant was John Parisella.

"The main thing John did for me," he said, "is he planted a seed. God put him in my life to plant a seed. He kept saying: 'You're going to be alright.'

"I never gave up because I knew that John worked through this early in his career. John was always encouraging to me; he was there for me. He always stayed in touch with me, checked on me to see if I was okay, and every time I talked to him, just kept telling me, 'You're going to be okay; You're going to get through this.'"

Margotta resumed training Thoroughbreds in 2010, and eight years later said, "I can't tell you how good my life is now. In my heart, the only reason I'm alive is because God knew my eighty-three-year-old mother needed somebody to take care of her, and plus, He wanted me to go out and share the good news that you can beat this, like John did for me.

"I love training horses and I love winning big races," he said. "I love it; that's my passion. There's only one thing I love more, and that's saving somebody's life or saving somebody the agony of going through what I went through. That supersedes the horses.

"It's important to know that, no matter what John Parisella went through and what John Parisella did, John Parisella helped save Anthony Margotta Jr.'s life. That is clear. God put him in my life for a reason."

Which explains, as well as anything, those daily Scripture texts. A friend, an ex-jockey, started sending Scripture messages to Anthony while Anthony was getting back on his feet.

"They were extremely helpful throughout my recovery," he said. "So after I got myself on solid ground, I said, 'Let me put together a list of people I think this would be helpful for.' I was taught to share with others what has been given me through The Lord Christ—to spread The Good News of the Gospel. I have a list of twenty-four, mostly family members and very close friends—people I think it will be helpful for. John happens to be one of them."

Anthony and John talked frequently by phone, and the conversation always included a discussion of the day's passage from Scripture. Anthony also often reinforced another message—"Remember the words of Jesus Christ: It's better to give than to receive."

"John Parisella was a very big giver, very good, very generous," Anthony said, acknowledging that those John helped didn't always acknowledge his help much less return the favor, which disappointed John after he left racing.

"John's ultimate score is when he gets to the Kingdom of Heaven," Anthony said. "See, God didn't forget any of those people John took care of, that he helped—me included. So, when he gets up there, he will have a good position with The Lord. John is a very good guy, a God-fearing man, and he's done a lot of good. That will be taken into consideration when he's in the Judgment Seat. And he'll be in good shape."

Those words echo what Msgr. Thomas Hartman of God Squad fame once told John.

Winner's Circle

Previous page: God Squad on TV *(photo illustration by SDW);* bugler David Hardiman; father and bride walking down the aisle; and Gabby and Robbie Vaughan reciting their vows before minister Brent Jones *(photos courtesy of John Parisella)*

God's Odds

GROWING UP ON LONG ISLAND, nine-year-old Tommy Hartman dreamed of becoming a big-league ballplayer. Or, just like John at one point in his youth, a priest. "When I hit .250 in baseball one year," he is said to have told newsman Dan Rather, "I said, 'Hmm, I better become a priest.'" Turned out to be a divine choice.

Tommy became Father Tom on May 29, 1971. That same year John Parisella saddled three hundred seven starters as a racehorse trainer, making a name for himself with 16.9% winners and 43% in-the-money finishers. Tommy and John didn't know each other then, and wouldn't meet for three decades.

During those thirty or so years, John interacted with an ever-widening circle of celebrities, while achieving noteworthy success as a trainer and experiencing what he called his "ups and downs." But even in his lowest times, John never stopped relying on God. "He's very religious," said the woman he called Bonnie. "I know he goes to church every Sunday. He does stuff like that."

> *My faith never wavered. I never stopped praying. I can't even tell you I stopped for three days. It's got me through my entire life of turbulence, when you get right down to it.*
>
> *I really felt it was God in my life. I got fired from two jobs; I couldn't ride a horse. What was I doing there? I fit nowhere else; I couldn't be a nine-to-five guy. I felt it was all His doing.*
>
> *I never went through rehab; God got me through it. I was*

able to go on with my career. I don't know how I held it together—I had ups and downs, but I still went on. I felt Jesus was always sending me messages.

Father Tom, meanwhile, served the parishioners at St. James in Seaford in Nassau County and later at St. Vincent de Paul in Elmont (home of Belmont Park). In 1979 he was persuaded to accept the position as head of Telecare, the television station of the Rockville Centre Diocese. He spoke openly of his love for "parish work," saying he particularly enjoyed the ministry of meeting people who had problems, those he called "people who thought they were alone."

April 1987 proved to be a momentous time for both men. On April 18, the day before Easter, John's Simply Majestic won the California Derby by ten lengths in track record time, setting off a frenzy about the horse's ineligibility for the Kentucky Derby. Days before, cable television station News 12 Long Island asked Father Tom to be part of a short feature about Easter and Passover. When told they needed a rabbi to pair with him, Father Tom suggested Marc Gellman, whom he "knew of" but didn't "know."

A short time later, Monsignor Thomas Hartman and Rabbi Marc Gellman launched the "God Squad" on Cablevision. The following year Simply Majestic broke Secretariat's world record for a mile and an eighth. After a decade on Cablevision, "God Squad" moved to Telecare and eventually was syndicated—reaching fifteen million homes per week at its peak. Around that time John set the record for most wins in one race meeting at Turfway Park.

Father Tom and Rabbi Gellman began writing a companion weekly column that was distributed nationally by Tribune Media, and co-authored several books, including "Religion For Dummies" and the children's titles "How Do You Spell God?" and "Where Does God Live?" They spoke at church and charitable events across the country, appeared regularly on ABC-TV's "Good Morning America" and were frequent guests on the "Imus in the Morning" New York City radio program. (Shock jock Don Imus would proclaim a "window of purity" or a "filth-free zone" whenever the God Squad duo were his guests. Imus once told listeners of Msgr. Hartman: "He's the only man on planet earth I can't say anything bad about.")

Their interfaith schtick was a mixture of serious discussion of religion and faith with good-natured ribbing and banter that served to bridge the gap between faiths. "We understood the fundamental obligation of friends, which was to find common ground and not to pursue things that would damage the friendship," Father Tom once said. "How we imagine God is different, but how we imagine what God wants us to do is exactly the same." Added Rabbi Gellman: "The credibility of our mission was not that he was handsome and I was funny. The credibility was that I was a working rabbi and he was a working priest."

As the God Squad duo spread their message, John was sharing his wealth—literally—in many ways. Helping others was how John lived. "If you and I were walking with John down the street—pick any city," said Ken Dunn, "and you saw a guy walking toward us who you could tell was a little down on his luck or a panhandler, there must be an aura about John because they always went right to him. And John always did something. I never saw him turn them away." Said Jimmy Clipboard: "John was the only trainer who had grooms and hot-walkers living with him."

A good example is the story of Tim Ritvo, as John told it:

I helped Tim out by allowing him to live rent-free at my home in New York while Kathy awaited a heart transplant at their home in Florida. After the successful operation, Tim lived rent-free in my home; I gave him a sports car to drive; and I had him live with me at Saratoga that summer—him and his son Michael, who I love and who loved hanging out with me—while Kathy was recuperating.

Tim owed the feed man sixty-eight thousand, which would have put him out of business. But I had great rapport with the feed guy so I okayed Tim that if he didn't pay, I'd make myself responsible. So he let Tim go on with his training operation.

Kathy Ritvo is one woman that I have the utmost respect and admiration for. Given one year to get a heart, she didn't get in until the last month. She's never stopped fighting. She'll always remain special in my eyes.

Years later, around 2009-2010, Morris Bailey pursued purchasing Gulfstream in Florida, and chose John to head the team to run the track if he succeeded. Recognizing Ritvo's knowledge of the racing game, John chose him to be his assistant. But Frank Stronach, who had tried to recruit John to be his trainer twenty years earlier, outbid Bailey for Gulfstream, and Ritvo eventually became chief operating officer of the Stronach Group for racing and gaming. John's assessment of Ritvo was validated; many feel Stronach and Ritvo saved horse racing through their strong management of the Stronach Group.

* * *

JOHN'S DAUGHTER GABBY WAS APPROACHING her teen years and John had befriended Anthony Margotta Jr. by the time he met Father Tom. John had generously helped others throughout his flamboyant, volatile career but more often than not felt those he helped were like the nine lepers who never came back to Jesus to thank Him after He had cured them. The soft-spoken priest was still living out the words he had spoken twenty years earlier: "meeting people who had problems, people who thought they were alone."

Max Kupferberg and Father Tom were on the Board of Directors of this bank together. I was training for the Kupferbergs then.

I was struggling with some things, and Max said, "Let me speak to Monsignor Hartman. Let's see if he'll meet with you."

Right away it was, like, God-sent. Once he came into my life, he raised the bar for me. I saw him every week.

It was meant for Father Tom to come into my life. If he didn't appear in my life, as strong as I might be with having Jesus in my corner, I don't know if I was THAT strong.

I was having so much resentment inside of me. It's no good. You have no life. He's the one who taught me; I'll never forget the statement he made:

"John, listen to me. You're blessed. You're a giver. Them not giving back doesn't mean anything, because Jesus is going to pay you back a hundred times over."

All of a sudden, that was my wakeup call. The resentment started to fly out of me. I was like, "That's a good return. I'm an edge player, and that's really good."

Father Tom's counsel was put to the test in 2015 when, out of the blue, Bethenny Frankel called her stepfather and extended an invitation or, depending on your point of view, made a request: a reunion staged as an episode of Real Housewives of New York City. "I had put her mentally in the back of my mind, that she didn't exist anymore," John said.

"John called me," Ted Sabarese said. "He was excited. He was going on her TV show. He was excited about going on the TV show and the opportunity to get back with her."

That meeting, which took place on a beach in Miami, was heart-wrenching for John and, emotional (in the true spirit of reality TV) for both.

Bethenny pulled no punches, reminding him of the sometimes chaotic, volatile environment in which she grew up. John expressed his regrets, acknowledged her success and expressed his pride in it. He told her she had, in effect, turned her back on him. She disputed it and said she thinks of him as the only father she ever knew.

John left that strange encounter sworn to never watch Bethenny on television—"It would hurt too much"—and not expecting to ever reconcile: "I don't matter to her." Two years later, though, John reached out, texting Bethenny to ask if she would attend Gabby's wedding.

> *I was sure Bethenny would not attend, but Gabby wanted to invite her. She wanted to invite all of the people she'd met who she thought were important in my life.*

The exchange of text messages, as John recalled, went like this:

JOHN: "Let me know if you don't so this way she (Gabby) won't be embarrassed by sending you an invitation."

BETHENNY (after John pressed for an answer): "Enough. You are beyond negative and I will not tolerate it. I do not know Gabby. I barely know you now. Stop this. I have had enough abuse."

Father Tom announced in 2003 that he had been diagnosed with Parkinson's disease, and retired from the God Squad in 2009. He died February 16, 2016, a few months short of his 70th birthday. John saw his friend and final mentor for the last time just before he passed away.

> *When I went to see him, the rabbi was there. It was the only time our paths crossed.*

> *Father Tom hadn't opened his eyes or acknowledged anyone for some time. I bent down, kissed him and said: "Tom. It's*

John, your horse trainer." He opened his eyes and smiled. Rabbi Gellman was shocked.

The prayer card made for Father Tom's funeral reads:

> A beautiful life
> that came to and end:
> He died as he lived,
> everyone's friend.
> In our hearts a memory always
> will be kept,
> of one we loved
> and will never forget.

John saddled the final winner of his training career three weeks later, and retired from racing that April. His final trip to the Winner's Circle was with a horse named Repent Twice. With his career behind him, John moved to northern California's Bay Area to be nearer to his daughter, and soon after received the news that Gabby would be getting married.

A Dream Come True

THE WEDDING OF GABRIELLE PARISELLA and Robbie Vaughan—on June 23, 2018 at Blackhawk Country Club in Danville, California—was one of the three most important events in John's life (after Gabby's birth and John kicking drugs). That's saying a lot, considering that the 6,770 races in his career included the Kentucky Derby, the Preakness, some Breeders' Cup events, countless stakes races coast to coast and Simply Majestic's world record-setting run. But no one who knew John disagreed, especially not his daughter.

"My dad dreamed about my wedding when I was a child more than I did," Gabby said. "I wasn't that girl who picked out my wedding dress before, or dreamt of what my wedding day would be like. I wasn't anti-wedding; I was just a jock and cared about sports when I was a kid. But he thought about it all the time. If I wasn't going to get married, it would have been sad for him not to see that. So I'm glad I found someone I wanted to marry."

Among the wedding guests were Rick Pitino, Ken Dunn, Jimmy Clipboard, John Nash, Bruce Levine and Scott Lake. They were there to honor the bride, for sure, but more so because they knew how much the day meant to her proud papa. "To me, that was an absolute honor," said Scott Lake. "It was a very select group from the racetrack." Said John Nash: "It was a beautiful wedding. I hope John doesn't have to pay for it for the next thirty years."

The walk down the aisle was punctuated by a friend's shout of "your biggest winner, John." John's bushy Italian eyebrows danced as he smiled broadly. As it is for nearly every bride and her father, that stroll was the culmination of all those years from infancy to adulthood that produced so many treasured memories. But instead of "Here Comes The Bride," the large wedding party (two maids of honor, six bridesmaids and their escorts) entered to "The Call to the Post," played by David Hardiman, the bugler at Golden Gate Fields. So much for weepy sentimentality.

"I got there and it was so festive," the new Mrs. Vaughan said of her big day. "It was awesome. I wrote everything down right away just so I don't forget anything."

Officiating was Brent Jones, an ordained minister who played tight end on three of the San Francisco 49ers' Super Bowl champs. Beginning on a light note himself, he said: "Usually we say face each other, but maybe we should say face off." In a nod to Robbie Vaughan's love of ice hockey, bride and groom grabbed hockey sticks and Jones proceeded to "drop the puck," after which he said: "Now this is a legendary wedding. You will never see one like this ever again. We've got a bugler; we've got a hockey face-off, and all we need now is a football player."

The three-time All-Pro and recipient of the Bart Starr Man of the Year Award in 1998 then conducted the wedding ceremony—as his daughter Courtney, the one quoted on the wedding website, looked on from her place in the wedding party. At one point Jones read from a well-worn Bible that had belonged to Gabby's maternal grandfather, World War II veteran William Endicott, who died just a few months before the wedding. "He and Gabby were very close," her mother said.

* * *

GABBY PARISELLA AND ROBBIE VAUGHAN MET as high school freshman, even though they attended rival schools. But it wasn't until they were in college that a friend brought them together and they began dating. Robbie concocted an elaborate ruse when he proposed marriage on July 6, 2017. Their wedding website related it sweetly:

> "Robbie knew that Gabby and her mom, Melissa, try their best to get up to Seattle every summer, but this year a trip wasn't planned. Robbie called Melissa and told her his proposal plan, so Melissa knew she had to get the trip in the books. His main goal was to surprise Gabby, which he thought he could accomplish by secretly flying to Seattle. Robbie booked a 6 am flight (an hour earlier than Gabby's flight) and his brother, Kevin, left his car in the airport parking lot with a picture of a written-out map of how to get to the car.
>
> "With an almost dead phone, Robbie drove north to Gabby's Grandma and Grandpa's house. When he got to the house, he built a path of fresh rose petals in the backyard. With the help of Gabby's mom, a photographer captured every moment, and two miniature ponies grazed in the backyard during the proposal. He made sure it was perfect.
>
> "As he waited for Gabby to arrive she had no idea this was going to happen. She had unbrushed hair and wore a shirt on with a hole in it. When she arrived at her Grandma's she gave the greeting she always did, but she didn't see her Uncle Steve. She asked where he was and her Grandma said, 'He's working in the backyard. Go say hi then we can have some Swedish pancakes.' This was a normal statement coming out of her mouth so Gabby obeyed. She opened the back door. She looked down and saw rose petals. As soon as she looked up, she saw Robbie walking towards her with his hands out.
>
> "He said, 'Hey Babe' and Gabby knew at that moment the day she had been dreaming of was coming true."

By then John had moved to Monterey, south of the Bay Area, to be nearer his daughter. He spent a year helping plan the perfect wedding.

"The whole wedding process was a lot of fun with him," Gabby said, "because he cared about every decision. He wanted everything to be perfect. It was almost more about how the outcome was for him than it was for me because I knew I was going to be fine because I found my forever person."

At the wedding dinner John told everyone, to cheers and rousing applause: "The man she found is as humble as she is, which I thought was impossible. She found a first-round draft pick."

*　*　*

JOHN'S REFLECTIONS ON HIS DAUGHTER'S WEDDING affirmed her take on it, even though they never compared notes.

The two most important things to me are, number one, that I was still around and able to walk her down the aisle, and, number two—not that it would have mattered to her, but—I was able to give her the kind of wedding I wanted for her.

Every day, I feel great about it.

Family Album

Gabrielle Parisella says of growing up with her dad three thousand miles away: "My unconventional pieces just fit together. I had a lot better childhood than a lot of people did with their parents both in the house." If, as the saying goes, a picture is worth a thousand words, here is a "7,000-word" look at moments in the life of John Parisella's daughter with her family. *(Photos courtesy of Melissa Sanders)*

John commissioned an artist in Saratoga Springs to paint "First Lead" —showing Melissa in the barn area, holding baby Gabrielle with Sam trailing behind.

Before Roxy, John and Melissa gave five-year-old Gabby a full-grown pony they named Merrylegs, who lived with her in California.

Gabby leads her horse "Classy" to her first riding lesson.

Gabby became an accomplished rider.

That's Grandma Lillian, John's mother, holding baby Gabby.

John and Gabby with Bishop John S. Cummins following her Confirmation.

Gabby's brother Sam, Melissa and John with Gabby at her graduation from Loyola Marymount University.

Through Others' Eyes

IT IS SAID THAT THE TRUE measure of a man's life is the way he is seen through others' eyes. In John Parisella's case, the views of many who were close to him through the years confirm the picture painted in the pages of his life story:

Rick Pitino: "John's one of the most complex people I've ever met in my life. He gets so high and so low. I've always tried to get him to have balance in his life. But he's so high or so low all the time. He would always live much bigger than he should have lived ... always lived day-to-day like a millionaire. And at times he had it, but he'd give it away, spend it. There's no such thing as buying savings bonds with John Parisella."

Gary Gullo: "John never held back. He went ninety-nine miles an hour all the way through. That's what John is. All the craziness aside, he's got a great heart and would help anybody."

Hall of Fame jockey Angel Cordero: "You need something, a big favor to meet somebody or get to somebody? If he don't know the person, he'll find somebody who does. He was not only a good trainer; he's a good human being. He's got a great heart. He will help anybody; that's what I love about him."

Trainer Scott Lake: "When you are his friend, you are his friend and he'll do anything for you."

Owner Morris Bailey: "He's a Brooklyn kid who came with his Brooklyn friends, his Italian friends, into the game. He had a cast of characters. A lot of them became trainers, and he, by far, was the best. He was dynamic and successful."

Owner Ted Sabarese: "John never had the blueblood owners with the big, big horses. A little because of that, and just John being John—he was always a nice guy, just sometimes difficult—he never got elevated to where he deserved to be. It's unfortunate that John never got the recognition he should have. He's a great horseman."

Racing executive Ken Dunn: "John had a very short fuse. You'd think he was 6-2 and 190 pounds and in great shape. But he wasn't. I've never seen him in a fight, but I've seen him go chest-to-chest with people he shouldn't."

Pro basketball executive and horse owner John Nash: "It's hard to be concise because there are several sides to John. Number one, he's an incredibly loyal friend. He will always take your side, even before he gets the details. His friends can do no wrong. He will defend them, and defend them aggressively—usually verbally, but whatever it takes. He has, to a fault, defended his friends without concern about his personal welfare. He would argue and create enemies of people that he might have needed over the years. But at that time it didn't matter. It was what was in the best interests of his friends. He always put his friends ahead of himself."

In the aftermath of his daughter's wedding, John reflected on people who helped him to be able to enjoy that day and their places in all that had gone before it.

> *Myself being an only child, Rick Pitino is the brother I never had, and he played an important role in my life ... During our nearly fifty-year friendship, Morris Bailey became a real estate icon but still continues to be there as a friend today ...*

Aside from my friendship with Father Tom, who happened to be one of the finest human beings on earth, his guidance helped me to become strong enough for me to throw my therapist out the window (not literally) ...

He even had kind words for his estranged stepdaughter.

Although Bethenny and I have not been able to reconcile, inside of me I still have the feeling of how proud I am for all she has accomplished—like any father would feel.

Shortly after the wedding John left northern California, where everyone was a stranger and only a few became, at best, casual friends. His free-spending ways and willingness to share whatever he had with so many others left him living modestly in retirement wherever he went.

Rick Pitino spent the 2018-19 basketball season in Greece, coaching the Panathinaikos team from Athens to the Greek Cup championship. Meanwhile his son Richard, head coach at the University of Minnesota, exacted the ultimate measure of revenge on his father's former team, eliminating Louisville in the first round of March Madness.

John communicated with Gabby virtually every day, as he had for years, and in January 2019 received joyful news: By mid-year he would be a grandpa.

Author's note

BECAUSE I GREW UP IN THE BLUEGRASS STATE, the Kentucky Derby entered my consciousness early—when California-bred Swaps won the 1955 Run for the Roses. I was not yet ten, and from then on the first Saturday in May was a very important date on every year's calendar. As a young sportswriter in Louisville a little more than a decade later, I learned how to write about horse racing from one of the best, Marvin N. Gay Jr. of *The Louisville Times*. I covered several Derbies, the most memorable one in 1968 when Dancer's Image became the only Derby winner ever to be disqualified, after testing positive for the banned anti-inflammatory drug Butazolidin (which later was allowed in racing). Seeing jockeys up close left an impression that has never left me: diminutive but the embodiment of sinew and toughness.

When Frank Vento approached me about writing this book, I had to admit to him that I had never heard of John Parisella—nor John's well-known stepdaughter, Bethenny Frankel. When Frank asked if I knew anything about horse racing, I assured him I did. Enough to write about a trainer, I said.

We both thought of this as a horse racing book at the outset. But quickly we both realized that John Parisella was much more than a horse trainer. He was a personality; some would say a character. He'd had a lifetime of celebrity adventures to go with a distinguished career on the backside. He indeed was, as actor Jack Klugman dubbed him, the "Trainer to the Stars."

And therein lie the challenge of writing this book. Racing is the backdrop, and an essential part of John's life. But this is, first and foremost, the story of a man and all the famous people he came to know over the course of a long, colorful life, one marked by hard falls and amazing recoveries, by tremendous low points and spectacular highs. Maybe it's two books in one. Whatever, John's story is not typical even for horse racing, a sport replete with Damon Runyon's favorites.

Writing a book as complex as this one requires the cooperation of many people. My deep appreciation goes out, first of all, to my subject, who sat for more than two dozen interviews during two nearly week-long visits plus numerous telephone calls. Obviously, this book doesn't happen without him and, above all, his openness in relating all facets of his life. Thanks also to all others who agreed to share stories about John and answer my questions, especially: Rick Pitino, Angel Cordero, Ted Sabarese, Ken Dunn, Morris Bailey, Anthony Margotta Jr. and John's daughter Gabby, her mother Melissa, and brother Sam.

Jimmy Alexander, who provided valuable reference material and many insights, will be especially remembered for the three-day driving tour of Brooklyn he piloted. The man navigated one-way streets, construction zones, double-parked cars and bumper-to-bumper traffic with remarkable aplomb, and patiently showed me everything I asked to see. In their historic Ballston Spa homestead with roots that trace back to the American Revolution, Karin and Brian Skarka were gracious hosts during my visit to Saratoga and the Museum of Horse Racing and Hall of Fame. Yochana Abramson was equally hospitable when she allowed me and others to stay at her home in Monterey and use it as the base for four days of interviews with John.

My very good friend Richard Nathan made possible a level of public records research that is hard to top, and the Equibase online racing database, a truly remarkable resource, provided an invaluable, race-by-race record of John's long and winding career. Another close friend and former newspaper colleague, Jim Delaney, provided invaluable counsel. And Frank Vento, whose idea this book is and who put his money where his mouth is, endured many spirited discussions as he offered input that made the book better.

If you wonder about the absence of direct quotes from the aforementioned Bethenny Frankel, it's because she declined, through a public relations representative, to be interviewed. "Thank you for reaching out," wrote Stephen Fertelmes of Jill Fritzo Public Relations in an email response to my request that had been sent to an email I was told was Bethenny's. "Unfortunately, Bethenny is not available to participate. As you can imagine, she receives so many great requests but simply cannot accommodate them all. Thanks for thinking of her!" Hence, Bethenny's part in John's saga is pieced together from a variety of sources.

As usual, the finished product reflects the work of two tremendously talented individuals, editor Jon Rizzi and designer Scott Johnson. How fortunate I am to work with both! And, to modify an old saw, last but always first in my life, my supreme thanks to my wife, Melanie, without whose fierce support and unfailing encouragement and patience, I could not have finished.

DENNY DRESSMAN is a former award-winning reporter, editor and senior executive who concluded a 42-year newspaper career in 2007. A member of the Denver Press Club Hall of Fame and a past president of both the Colorado Press Association and the Colorado Authors' League, he is the author of nine other books. His biography of the late Grambling football coach, Eddie Robinson, in the context of Jim Crow segregation and the Civil Rights Movement of the early 1960s, was a Colorado Book Award finalist. He lives in Denver with his wife Melanie.